I NAME ME NAME

ALSO BY OPAL PALMER ADISA

Eros Muse, poems and essays
Until Judgement Comes, stories
Caribbean Passion, poems
Leaf-of-Life, poems
It Begins with Tears, novel
Tamarind and Mango Women, poems
Bake-Face and Other Guava Stories, stories

OPAL PALMER ADISA

I NAME ME NAME

PEEPAL TREE

First published in Great Britain in 2008
Peepal Tree Press Ltd
17 King's Avenue
Leeds LS6 1QS
UK

ISBN 13: 9781845230449

Peepal Tree gratefully acknowledges Arts Council support

ACKNOWLEDGEMENTS

Some of these poems have appeared in the following journals and anthologies:

Nexus; Obsidian II; The Caribbean Writer; Adam of Ifè, (ed. Naomi Long Madgett, Detroit: Lotus Press, 1992)*; I Hear a Symphony,* (eds Paula Woods & Felix Liddell, New York: Anchor, 1995)*; Transnacionalidad El Caribe y su Diàspora – Lengua, Literatura y Cultura en los Albores del Siglo XX; Meridian; MaComère, Gathering Ground* (eds. Toi Derricotte & Cornelius Eady, Ann Arbor: University of Michigan, 2006); *An Eye For An Eye Makes the Whole World Blind: Poets on 9/11* (eds. Allen Cohen & Clive Matson, Oakland, CA: Regent Press, 2002); *Words Upon the Waters* (ed. Karla Brundage, Oakland, CA: Jukebox Press, 2006)

The following essays have been previously published:

"A Barrel of Laughter and a Bucket of Tears", *Journal of Multicultural Heartspeak,* 1. 4, May 1997 <http://asilithejournal.com/ASILI/VOL-UMES/Vol1_4_may97.pdf>

"A Teller of Tall Tales: in Memory of Toni Cade Bambara", *Papyrus* 2.4, 1996: 12–13. The version in this collection has been revised.

"Children Must be Seen and Heard", in *Voice, Memory, Ashes* (eds. Jacob Ross & Joan Anim-Addo, London: Mango Publishing, 1999), pp. 25–42. The version in this collection has been revised.

"Life Outsmarting Death", *MaComère* 3, 2000: 5–7.

"She be the Spit and the Flame: June Jordan", *MaComère* 5, 2002: 1–5.

"She Scrape she Knee: the Theme of my Work", in *Caribbean Women Writers* (ed. Selwyn R. Cudjoe, Calaloux Publications, 1990), pp. 145–150.

"There is Always a Way: Gifted my Mother's Maxims", *Looking Back*, (ed. Rebecca Wecks, Aptos, CA: New Brighton Books, 2003), pp. 74–84.

"A Man to Lean On, a Friend to Hang With", *Journal of Multicultural Heartspeak* 2.4, November 1997/February 1998 <http://asilithejournal.com/ASILI/VOLUMES/vol2_1_nov97_feb98.pdf>

Special thanks to Devorah Major, Giovanni Singleton and Doug Scott for pointing out large and small things that help me to make the work stronger, special thanks to Steve Jones for layout of the graphic poems, and especially to Kamau Brathwaite for his keen insights.

Gratitude also to *The Caribbean Writer*, its editorial board and staff who have been great supporters of my work.

Blessings also to Jeremy & Hannah for their vision and making sure that Caribbean writers have an outlet to share and distribute their work.

CONTENTS

PART I: POEMS

PART II: PROSE

POSTSCRIPT: TRIBUTES

Dedicated to:

People throughout the world who are struggling to create better lives for themselves, but especially for the people of Haiti and South Africa

and also to:

Dr. Barbara Christian, a sister/friend and mentor
(1943–2000)

&

Reginald Lockett, a brother/poet who knew laughter
(1947–2008)

PART I

POEMS

i am the i am the same i that is child of catherine and orlando i that is the granddaughter of edith &
ezekiel and anita & richard i am the what of which has yet to be defined i and i womanfari chanting up
humanland the i and i calling on jahmoda i as in collective as in not
standing along as inbelonging to a lineage jahmoda i and i but
the colonialist warned me dot my i's innocentlyi go back
and apply the tittle feeling insular isolated ignored yet
intrepid my egothe self that is i i as in singular i that is
a pronoun the 9th letter of the roman alphabet the 9th
letter of the english alphabet i that comes from an isle
a much smaller place than an island i that is an illegal
ignorant intractable immigrant that i belongs to
babylon but i dwell in humanland

i identity i lineage i group not tribe as a racist pejorative
not chief as the derogative demotion i as in i know
who i am i insist on being myself even when others
scoff mei and i before now before then not a pronoun
not an icon between you and i not the i that stands
alone the i that is assured the i that know i was
imported to work the cane-fields to accept the rapist
into my bed to bear and love his child to not be a
witness but to be the witness this i that i am declares
unequivocally it is i who else can it be but ii yes i i and
i i chant down babylon i morph i transform i
transgress the very notion of i i secularize i sanctify i
scant i skank i scandalize the i that is i that insert I self
i words i thoughts i ideas through i body not the
plural form of i but the singular i i body becomes the
script upon which i identity is written i body that
cannot be taken from i not through theft war abduc-
tion enslavement forced labor rape i body remains i
and i cannot be baptized out of me cannot be
separated from i continental roots cannot be
anybody's body but i and i the ithat is the i that is the
i even when taunted on the streets by careless lads and
lustful men who wanted me to hate this body bursting
forth in womanly splendor i that was that girl that was
fearful grew to see iself i touch iself i consent to have
others touch the self that was i not always loving either
i who was innocent and irreverent i who was injured and
insubordinate i and i chant iself up the self that is i i was once
now i am i am who knows i am who knew i am who will know i know
i own knowing the i that i am i am an incisor gnawing my way i am i i seeking independence i the
intellectual i self the iness of i i the internet and the instant message I not yet invented i looking at the
eye seeking i the i that i am i am i and i the womanfari i the i and i jahmoda i i

I

i am   the   i am
the same i that is child of catherine and orlando
i that is the granddaughter of edith & ezekiel
and anita & richard
i am the what of which has yet to be defined
i and i womanfari   chanting up humanland
the i and i calling on jahmoda
i as in collective   as in not standing alone
as in   belonging to a lineage
jahmoda   i and i

but the colonialist   warned me   dot my i's
innocently i go back and apply the tittle
feeling insular isolated ignored
yet intrepid
my ego   the self that is i   i as in singular
i that is a pronoun
the 9th letter of the roman alphabet
the 9th letter of the english alphabet
i that comes from an isle
a much smaller place than an island
i that is an illegal   ignorant   intractable   immigrant
that i belongs to babylon but i dwell in humanland

i identity i lineage i group
not tribe as a racist pejorative   not chief as
the derogative demotion
i as in   i know who i am
i insist on being myself even when others scoff at me   i and i
before now   before then   not a pronoun
not an icon
between you and i   not the i that stands alone
the i that is assured

the i that knows i was imported to work the cane-fields
to accept
the rapist into my bed   to bear and love his child
to not be a witness
but to be the witness
this i that i am declares unequivocally   it is i
who else can it be   but i   i   yes i   i and i
i chant down babylon   i morph   i transform
i transgress
the very notion of i i secularize   i scantify   i scant   i skank
i scandalize   the i that is i that insert   i-self
i   words   i   thoughts   i   ideas
through i body not the plural form of i   but the singular   i
i body becomes the script upon which i identity is written
i body that cannot be taken from i   not through theft   war
abduction   enslavement   forced labour   rape
i body remains   i and i
cannot be   baptized out of me
cannot be   separated   from i continental roots
cannot be anybody's body but   i   and i
the i   that is the i   that is the i
even when taunted on the streets
by careless lads and lustful men
who wanted me to hate this body
bursting forth in womanly splendour
i that was that girl
i that was fearful   grew to see i-self
i touch i-self   i consent to
have others touch the self that was i
not always loving either
i who was innocent   and irreverent
i who was injured   and insubordinate
i   and   i chant   i-self up
the self that is   i
i was once   now i am
i am who knows

i am who knew
i am who will know   i know
i own knowing the i that i am
i am an incisor   gnawing my way

i am i
i seeking independence
i the intellectual
i self the i-ness of i
i the internet and the instant message
i not yet invented
i looking at the eye seeking i
the i that i am

i am
i and i
the womanfari i

the i and i jahmoda

i
i
i

THE TONGUE IS A DRUM

the tongue is a drum
      a drum
            a drum
the tongue is a drum
and drumming
         has been outlawed

         no drumming allowed
except on sundays
in a few public parks
between the hours
of 2 and 4 p.m.

the tongue is a drum
      a drum
         a drum
and drumming
has been forbidden
         especially
              if you're non-white
         especially
            if you're female
              the drum is
                    forbidden

these are not
stories to scare
        i tell
too many lost
their tongues
when they insisted
      on speaking
when they
      defied authority

when they
        demanded their rights

the tongue is
        a drum
                a drum
and drumming isn't allowed
not any more

                not even on Sundays
                in the park

but my tongue
is ancient/communication
it doesn't
take orders
very well
                it keeps learning
                        new languages
                it creates
                        new syntaxes

the tongue is
        a drum
                a drum
and the drum
        is an ancient art form
                that reaches all the people
no matter the distance
no matter the interference

the tongue insists
        on being a drum
                and the drum
        sounds
                budum-budum

                              loud
continuous
             echoing
throughout
the distance

the tongue
        is a drum
                  a drum
                           budum
                                       budum
budum

UNDERSTANDING MY STORY: PHYLLIS WHEATLEY

i   had another name
a   name given to me
by   my mother and father
a   name that connected me
                            to my people

i was   only eight years old
                            when captured
                            when made to swallow
                            jesus whole

i perfected
their prayers
forgot   to remember
my name
until i wrote
i love   me and my own
still

i   am known only as
                            phyllis wheatley
                            my owners
                            were wealthy
                            they schooled my memory
                            to be in their image

don't you think
i looked for my mother

longed for my sister

dreamed my father
would come and claim me

but   no one
came to get me
no   one

the benevolent wheatleys

taught my fingers
to lace thread
my mouth
to parrot words

thanks for saving me
the black primitive
from damnation
thanks for your generosity
thanks for your superiority

i was their little monkey

but i was no monkey

i surprised them
with i own verses
my imitation so perfect
it surpassed their own

still the attacks
from my own are fists in my chest

what is the nature
of your accusation
do you want to know my fear
do you care to acknowledge my longing
can you fathom

my singularity

i   phyllis
                         i value i words
                         i black woman
                         i writer of religious and moral poems
                         i book published in1773
                         i insist on being known

i   survived to tell
i   story

PEELING OFF THE SKIN: NAT TURNER

i — nat turner as ghost

i would do it again
plot and plan
and kill too
if pushed
would confide
in my betrayer
hoping to win
his heart
to his own
heart beat

> i would do it again
> work my way
> through the hatred
> cover my skin
> with promise's voice
> squeeze through the
> fear until i find
> a breath in which
> to seed one dream

yes
i would do it again
and again
until i see a glint
of a smile snagged
on doubtful lips
and for one black child
to glance unshackled
at the moon

> i would be the ghost

        that prodded their steps
        to head north
                i would be the wind
                that called them to
                my bosom

yes
i would do it again
and i do

ii — nat turner as purse

pressed against
her body
my smooth searing
is the ache
that is her heart
      since she came south
           wife to a man
                who loves breaking things
      she has long been shattered
           shards glued into newness
now he presses
my thighs to her chest
me   a man made fugitive
      we must both endure
           his caresses
      revenge and perversion
           this impotent voyeur
           the husband
who sometimes
      goes to her bed
      lawfully assured
           she will bow down
afraid to run
afraid to be free

but she
lives the underground
railroad
        through me

i come   between
        them
my skin   the wall
that damns their offspring
through whom
i live on
        and on

iii — nat turner as lamp shade

in destroying
he illuminates
blinded by my blackness
my skin lights
        the freedom
he can never penetrate

        i am the runaway
        god in massa's parlour
                listening to the talk

his habits
stored in my hue
next time
i will know
        next time

each night
he sits to read

                his eyes grow dimmer
                        but i shine/memory
                                that will never fade

my skin stretched taut
enduring the heat
        of the flame
                licking my time

FOREMOTHER I: MARY PRINCE (1788?–1833)

fi me story cannot
begin at the beginning
the genealogy too long

but let me tell you
the truth now
tired won't see tomorrow

me did born into bondage
at brackish pond
one foolish man

think him own me
as if me could belong to someone
when me little like tree stump

him sell me from out of
me mammy's arms
me tell you another thing

eye-water don't know sadness
but i wouldn't mind him
him beat me   him touch-touch

me up   him spit pan me
nothing don't left for him do me
but him could never

make me believe him over me
and him know so him decided
fi mek me suffer

sell me again to grand turk
place me never know about
but spite was me weapon

me would never give him
the satisfaction fi see me
pan me knees begging mercy

better salt eat me flesh
to bones   better me dead
still owning me own chest

back and forth him send me
bermuda   licks
antigua   kicks

but me still own meself
marrying who me love
feeling free as dove

mammy always in me heart
biding me time smart
never giving in or surrendering

FOREMOTHER II: MARY SEACOLE (1805–1881)

from i was a little girl
my feet itched at the water's edge
watching the waves ebb
ships coming and going

i observed my mother
sniffing and sorting herbs
forever blending and tasting
her brow knitted in concentration

find your gift she insisted
help someone   be star or lantern
my hands carried the moon
even when night was dark

i would not be land-bound
robbed by womanly constraints
oh panama i come   fingers   liniment
sleep on clean sheets and stomachs well fed

there is and always will be a difference
between a woman and a lady but i was both
my face and heart unveiled to every man
my bedroom   eden before the fall

i was persuasive   i could charm
and not even a misguided nightingale
would deter me from administering
what i know to ally and enemy equally

i would leave treasure map for daughters
who would surely follow on my heels
listening keenly to the winds that beckoned them
herbal plants stored securely in their suitcases

SAY MY NAME

I

born in the land we called xairu
meaning beautiful
like all the women
me saartjie
daughter of the khosian people
chant i name
i shout it so the wind
can take it back
to my people

II

when food was scarce
and i was only twenty
i travelled to cape flat
worked as a farm hand
hoping against hope
but still only sweat
dripped from my brow
boring a hole in my heart

then marriage promised
seeking protection
accepted and travelled
to england
only to find a cold country
inhabited by ghosts
who gawked and pointed
scrutinizing every inch
of my body
mouth pried open

buttocks prodded
legs pulled apart
private passage
measured and pinched
my heart now a cavern

i chanted i name
saartjie
days-after-months-after years
more than four years
i suffered aliases

saartjie
saartjie
i chanted
i am life   i am alive

III

me   saartjie
i loose i-self
removed from my people
paraded naked
at piccadilly fair
shame became i name

too weary to hold
i-self
heart removed
i was renamed
venus hottentot
i spirit hovered
while i crawled
alcoholism   prostitution
i no longer had i-face

IV

not even death freed me
i body replicated
brain and genitalia
pickled and displayed
i spirit shrilling out
i am saartjie
saartjie baartman
not venus hottentot
saartjie

V

long last
i back in i skin
stretched out
at the gamtoos river
i once more i-self
i name called me back

i-self free
i body i own again
i name saartjie
i name
saartjie baartman
i inna i-self again

FINDING I-SELF

sometimes we stumble
and are picked up

sometimes someone
singles us out of the crowd

sometimes we nominate ourselves
but most times

we are called
by an inner knowing
and although
we might shuffle
act as if we don't know
we knew all long

i knew from inside the womb
i had something immense to do

you do too
but you keep running
from it
keep looking around
as if it isn't you
who is being called

you cannot disappear in the crowd
you have been named
you have been identified
you are being awaited

just pick yourself up
pin yourself like wet garments
on a clothes-line

allow the breeze
to dry you fragrant

and be the self that is knowing
the self that answers

here i am
i am present

CHARCOAL
(for elaine kim)

I

breathe deeply

> when california
> still belonged
> to the ohlone people
> each year
> they would set
> the meadows on fire
> > stimulate growth

II

breathe deeply

> some traditions
> pile the dead body
> of a loved one
> and set it aflame
> witnessing
> the bones whitening
> > in the heat

III

breathe deeply

        on occasions
        fire becomes necessary
        the kiln burnishing
        pottery to store
        the clan's history
        cooking meals
        charring bodies
        a bonfire

IV

breathe deeply

a cross burning   a lynching
free-burning   tarred bodies
slow-burning   five children alone
ember   cinder   cold   trapped

incandescent   ebullient

V

after the body burns
and the flames cool
family comes
gathers the ashes
stores it in a jar
places it on an altar

you too must
sort through
the soot
that was once   your home
gather   memories
you   survivor

VI

many years from now
bent with old age
when you stop to rest
your arthritic knees
on a park bench
a memory will dance
before your eyes
that small trinket
you treasured
the givers smell at the giving
and anger will rise in you

that fire
that darn fire
thief
murderer
anarchist

PAN-AFRICANISM

tribal songs
echo throughout
        voodoo tents
                rum bars
                        disco floors
        pocomania meetings
                jazz flute sessions

ancestral idioms
believed
to be forgotten
get played over in
        double-dutch
                hambone
        the shuffle
                high five

tongues
form
olodumare syntax

                all over
                        the diaspora
                we shine
                        the same sweat

                history grafted
        in our fingerprints

DEMOCRATIC PROCESS

history
        stammers
                a linguistic slip

blood oozes
                perspiration
                        on the dance floor
                blades against gods
        skin against epigrams

                massacre decorates the hill
                poppies floating in the flood

transistor radios
        for sterilization

                the homeless
                        clean windshields

election
on the way

AMANDLA: FOR WINNIE MANDELA

we might
not be able
to turn
stone into bread
water into wine
but we knead
oppression into struggle

        we are
        magicians
        whose voices
        eclipse time
        our endurance
        breaks walls

but
for our vigilance
but
for our love
nelson mandela
wouldn't even
be a memory
much less
the quiver
that shakes the ground

        we are amandla
        we are victory

this parasite
that's striving
to suck us clean
will be pulled up
acid thrown
at its roots

we are fearless
as winnie mandela

who was more
than wife
        she freed nelson's voice
                crossed barricades
                        for her people

                all of us
                here and there
                are fighting
                like albertina sisulu
                mother of south africa
                climbing steadfast
                to keep the pest
                from stripping
                us to bone

CARRYING MOST OF THE WORLD

some women
of west africa

carry 30 pounds of yam
on their heads
baby tied
on their backs
basket in one hand
water jar in the other

others
carry loads of sticks
permanently bent
a strap slung across
their foreheads
which leaves an indentation

many
bow low to men
roles circumscribed
in a land where men
are gods

they serve husbands
eat what's left
vigorous workers
who move with grace

marking time
until...

SPEAK AND SPEAK AND SPEAK AGAIN

(in memory of audre lorde)

I

clear your throat
     lift your tongue
     that's lying heavy inside
     your mouth

press it against your teeth
     swallow the saliva
     gluing your jaws shut
     open your mouth

hear the words
     gurgling in your stomach
feel them climbing up
     seeking light and air
spit them out

silence offers   no reward
silence is   never silent

the words not spoken
     give you headache
     a gnawing pain
     in your stomach
     knots in your shoulder blades

silence stalks you
     a jack-in-the-box
silence
     slams doors in your face
silence
     leaves scars on your body

silence

> with the stroke of a pen
> dooms your children's fate
> blurs your face

words   need you

> smell them

they live inside you

> in those dark sweet places
> only your lover and children know

words   charge you

> grow them in your womb
> let them be born from
> between your brown thighs
> suckle them at your breast
> name them
> name them

II

when your tongue   touches the skin
> of your lover & your child

when your tongue   massages
> flesh & fold
> and sends a prayer

when your tongue   tongues words

you will taste   how bittersweet
> feelings are

you will discover   who you are
> whose flesh you'll tongue
> what words you'll tongue

III

my poetry bleeds outrage

>   at the men who abducted
>   that young sister
>   from the macarthur bart station
>   used & flushed her life
>
>   at those young brothers
>   in south l.a. who shot the blood
>   three times
>
>   at the man who sexually abused
>   both his step-daughters
>   one only fourteen
>   then found god & got off
>   with only five years probation

i run my words   through the rinse cycle
                      twice
                      add fabric softener

but my words   are still rough   gritty
                      their fresh fragrance
                      dissipates in the air

i am left with angry words
                      that don't heal wounds
                      comfort mothers' grief
                      or return a stolen life

my jaws begin   locking up
                      shutting in on themselves

IV

my tongue   drowning in spittle
                 stutters
my tongue   pushes against teeth

muscles   relax
my mouth   opens
                 words stumble out

        there is not
        silence
        there is not
        silence

language   is my reward

words

my very own

THE PAINTER
(for lloyd walcott)

he came into
our home
with furrowed brows
     seeking in his sister
     the parent
     he never had

this man   my uncle
looking nothing
like my mother
     no ready smile
     no burnt cork skin

     just a tentative artist

who knew the smell
of the kitchen
the feel of a knife
that unfolds a cabbage
     as well as acrylic brushes
     on canvas

     it wasn't his desire
     to prepare food
     for the rich to savour
     or to take on a wife
     or sire sons & a daughter
     who might need his support

all he really wanted
was to paint the landscape
so others might notice it
sketch tubby women

languishing under domesticity
carve gods from wood
and be an artist

MOTOWN

no one told michael
that he *got to be there*
for himself
that his face
was his godself
looking out into the world

michael sure enough
can sing and dance
command worldwide attention
don't stop until you get enough
performances
but did he get enough
mama's love and papa's love

does michael
love himself   love himself
cause *it does matter*
if you're black or white
it always mattered
and michael
you matter too
your once flat nose
chocolate skin
and nappy hair
you   michael
are that caterpillar
that never made it to a butterfly

i just want to kiss
your old face
we loved you
as you were

as you were
and you were divine
you were divine
and *i want you back*

DEAR AUDRE (LORDE): A LETTER

a male student   young enough to be my son
but too young to understand the significance
of america's invasion of grenada in 1983

yet full of rage bellows:
fuck that shit; women have choices
racism is real; sexism is feminist bullshit

should i drop him from my class
report him to his coach
or help him to understand what he denies?

two female students from the same class
confide during office hours
about being raped by mother's boyfriend

then kicked out the house
beaten up by an ex-boyfriend
        enacting your *transformation from silence*

you continue to reach out your hand
to me wherever you are
in the bosom of brown soil

manure for callaloo
sweetening a canestalk
or regulating the waves

THE DETROIT RIVER

my sorrow flows
like menses

the cries and accusations
of those who got tangled

under my dress
gnash at me

i carried as many
as i could

safely in my lap
even when feet were swollen
arms fallen boughs

i couldn't save all
hounds barking
at my banks

but i did
my part
i did

MR. DETROIT

dressed in lime-green shirt
and a teal-coloured suit

he is the remnant
of a city forgotten

under steel and a
defunct car industry

a city that reeked of jazz
fleeing the blues

he ain't stuck on sorrow
his daddy taught him

how to make an art
of misery

boy, listen here
he instructed

make sure you match
from your drawers

to your shoes
kill them with style

he's as real
as you can get

in a city halfway between
dying and vassalage

FROM FATHER TO SON

(in memory of philip farrar)

he had wooden legs
      walked strong with a cane
reared his son   to stand up
showed him   that feet
      were the heart
         and resolution the director

he carried a gun
      took no crap
not from anyone
when some white boys   tried to run him over
tried to tell him   he was nothing
he took out his pistol
      and shot out their tyres

he knew the ground
      on which he stood

his son grew
expecting steep roads
but knowing   feet are hearts
and walking   leads to a destination

A SONG OF PRAISE

(for neville & karl)

don't know why   they don't see you
cause you always   been there
been around   doing the same thing
      for your woman
      your children
      your friends
      the community

you man   deep chocolate

you man   sandy brown

you man   yellow

you man   nutmeg

you always been there

i've seen you
      child raised
          on your shoulder

i've seen you
      apron round
          your waist
          cooking up a storm

i've seen you
      bending
          in your garden
      your hands yielding
      vegetables to nourish

i've seen you
        tickling your wife
                laughing into her
        eyes   faithful
                        working every day
                sometimes   two jobs

don't know
why they say   you don't exist

cause i be seeing you
        all the time
                all over the place
doing the same thing
        being a real good man

KNOWINGNESS

women
who embrace   the warrior
                in themselves
        the roll of their
             backsides
        as they walk

who delight   in smelling themselves

rather than praying   on bent knees
      to the ghost on the cross

who love the texture   of kinky hair

know how to carve out
a space for themselves

such women
who refuse   hot-comb or sperm
to secure a job

who live family
protest apartheid/racism
in south africa/the usa
oppression
all over the world

know
        loving and keeping
        the fires burning
        turn into milestones

SISTERS BEHIND BARS

(for the women in fci-dublin)

sister
i call you
  who could be
  should be
the woman next door
i shout to look out
for my children
while i run to the store

you could be
should be
  the one i call howdy to
  as i work in my garden
  or sweep the garbage that people
  litter in front of my gate

sister
it's you i've been missing
the friendly face that greets
me when i arrive at work
or holds the door for me
  it is your story i haven't heard
  your sweet-pot i haven't tasted

sister
it's you i've been missing
in the lunch room
where we relax and shout out
girl i hear you

it's you i've been looking for
        in the church pew sitting beside me
        on the dance floor
        to give a high five as you bump me

sister   your children
        are being shuffled
        from foster home to relatives
        seeking you and not finding comfort
        crying at nights   during the day
        their eyes   a hunger
        food will never satisfy

sister
locked up
working for a dollar a day
without benefits or retirement plan
i'll not allow you to be forgotten
i'll carry you in my words

        for your children
        for your parents
        for yourself

BLACK WOMAN II
(for anita hill)

some would
have us believe
it was harmless flirtation

at best   a compliment
at worst   poor judgment

but how to keep smiling
when your boss
is telling you the
deeds of his penis

how to scream
when you've been trained
to defer to your supervisor

how to curse
when you have been reared
to be a lady and guard certain silences

clarence thomas   is judge for life

he will condemn
your daughter   to a back alley
abortionist

he will dismiss
your son   tell him to pull himself up
by his own boot strings

he won't care
your son   has no boots

clarence thomas will never
hear the screams   of your mother
your aunt or   your cousin darlene

          his patrons rule this land
          he's become the american dream
          a male
          accustomed   to women submitting

his sexist exploitation
is rendered   a lynching
          the group rallies to his aid

your silencing
is applauded
                    shut up the bitch

NOT ON OUR BACKS

(for barbara christian)

no
you cannot stand on my back
nor hers either
nor that sister's over there
our backs are not for rent anymore
not for the men in our lives
not even for our children
so no   god damn it
you cannot stand   lean   and don't even think about
using our backs as a step-ladder
we are not your strength   we are our own strength
we do not want to keep playing
harriet or sojourner or ida or fannie
not even bessie or lady day or dorothy
they did it for us

no   god damn it
you cannot stand on my back
not my sister's or my mother's
not my cousin's or even the whore's on the corner
you cannot stand on any of our backs
no   not anymore

we take charge of our own strength
we relinquish high blood pressure
we abandon obesity and breast cancer
we throw off madness
and chewing our own tongues   until we choke

we are god damn tired

are you deaf?
these words are spoken with love

i'll go to no more posthumous celebrations
to honour black women
who have worked themselves to death
left as they were alone to hold back the river
to set off the explosives and take the heat

no   step back
get off our backs
we black women have had enough
we are saving our energies and using our commitment
towards our own salvation

don't admire or look to us for strength
        go unearth your own
don't applaud us for being so capable
        when you didn't even bother
        to show up at the negotiating table
don't thank us
        when you failed to speak up in our defence
        or lend us your support

no more

        we black women are not going to give our lives
        for you anymore

we have learned to love ourselves
and we are not choosing death
we have decided on life
long and sun-filled
we are speaking up for ourselves
and we'll speak on your behalf too
but only if we are assured
we can count on you

too many strong black women have died
       way too young
              from cancer
from heartbreak
       from diabetes
from stress
       from lack of love
from obesity
       from disappointment
from the glass ceiling
       from being overworked
              from taking on everyone's load
from volunteering too much
       from being the one to organize the protest meeting
              from not being able to say no
              from giving too much of themselves
without receiving anything in return
from carrying sojourner's and harriet's
and ida's and fannie's
and bessie's and lady day's and dorothy's burden

no   god damn it
you cannot stand on my back
too many of my sisters have paid with their lives

no
you cannot stand on my back
       nor hers either
       nor that sister's over there
       our backs are not for rent anymore

STEADFAST

(for deeann)

sometimes
we have to take several steps
    backward
    go a round-about route
just to get
    where
we've always known
we were intent on arriving

sometimes
hanging back
    dilly-dallying
    shows you more clearly
the dream you   have been dreaming
            but could never remember

if you had walked straight
and not wandered
off the track
    you'd have missed
those splendid white orchids

CUT FROM THE SAME CLOTH

(for najuma)

not every woman
can raise a daughter
to find her own footprints
and walk with pride

      not every woman
      can raise a daughter
      who will nurse her through illness
      and help her to reach the other side

not every woman
can raise a daughter
to part from clan and tradition
and stand alone and find herself
a place where peace abides

      not every woman
      knows how to negotiate
      between the past and the present
      not every woman
      can love a daughter
      when she seldom
      experienced love

not every woman
knows how to open herself to love

PRAYED UP

their hands know
the heavy hour of labour
        the smell of onion
        the thorn of cotton

the preacher drones

                        repent sinners
                        go to your god
                        on bended knees

their hands have
scrubbed washboards
hot-combed hair
to soften stubbornness
born in geography
have slapped legs until
      i'm sorry ma'am
        ain't gonna do it again
is a chanting plea

                        heads bowed
                      in supplication
                      for what sins
                      do they seek
                      forgiveness?

arthritic hands
lotioned   nails trim
sit on their laps
in practiced submission

as they beseech again
but never for themselves

SEEKING PEACE

in the quiet of
the kitchen
where only the whirr
of the fridge can
be heard
the din of my
murdered son
hangs on the wall
while i cook another meal
i will not taste

on whom can i call?
where to buy ammunition?
      there is no red cross on the roof
      no demarcation
           between allies & enemies

in the heat of the battle
bullets resound
but the only sound i hear
is the gentle cry
of my child
no longer
strapped on my back

DINNER TIME

(for all people who are combatting hunger)

I

every day
there is at least
      one starch   two vegetables
      one lean meat   organically grown fruits
      and bottled water on my table

hungry does not live
in my home
hungry has never knocked
on my door
hunger is not even   a long-lost relative

but every day
somewhere in the world
        a mother places her pencil-sized child
        to flat breasts
hunger is constant

every day
somewhere in the world
        men keel over
        ribs sticking out
thirst is constant

every day
somewhere in the world
    children scavenge
    through garbage
need is constant

II

i can't imagine
my daughter so thin
          the wind could blow her down
i can't envision my son
          stomach bloated as a soccer ball
i can't conceive of my breasts
          so worn only pus drips from them
i can't recognize my man
          body a weather-battered twig

every day
like clockwork
some of us consume ourselves numb

ENOUGH

unable to move
> weighted down by what the news offers up
> people displaced
> lands ruined
> bodies decapitated

> trying to make sense of it
> wanting to believe
> someone learned something

the war rumble
raises tiny hairs on my arms
this well-fed nation
sitting arrogantly
on its throne
insisting on
creating the world
in its own image

despite the body-bags
bearing her sons
the outcry from the rest of the world

haven't we learnt anything since
> slavery
> the holocaust
> hiroshima
> cuba
> vietnam
> the sixties
> el salvador
> grenada

nicaragua
panama
iran
iraq

    i rise from my bemusement
    draw a world
    and name it peace

SAFE

(for rodney king & kathryn rashidi)

are you   safe
at home
with dead-bolts & burglar bars   safe
your safety-deposit box   safe

are your children at school   safe
am i woman   safe
are black men   safe
are citizens of every nation   safe
is my tongue   safe

is rodney king   safe
are haitians & mexicans   safe
are police & soldiers   safe
is my native land   safe

when the iron bird
whirs its machine noise
hovering over cities
casting glaring lights

                                        no safety

when their rage and victimhood
despondence   no jobs
detonate in the streets

                                        no safety

but i insist
name me   safe

NOT IN MY NAME

nestled in history
the eye hides
the film of its witness

after the earth
writhes from
warheads jammed
inside her sweet womb

after more men die
       in the name of country
       religion
       political ideology

after
       women are widowed
       children orphaned
       a community bereft of half of its labour force

even after
       mass exodus
       refugee camps
       too many bodies to count

what will be gained?

power must
concede to truth

justice must
prostrate before humanity

and daily each of us
must disavow war
in all our private spaces
and embrace peace globally

LAST THOUGHTS: 9/11 VOICES

all atrocities
are piled on the pyre
. of history
this is no different

Woman I

i must keep moving
how will he know
the cake has been ordered

that i didn't forget
it was to have been a surprise
a truce offering

fifteen years old and all we do now is fight
his pants too big and hanging
his music blasting vulgar lyrics

merciful lord
spare me to tell him
i love you my only son

i love you
mercy mercy
my body's on fire

the morning of the terror
is still too new
to · reflect on the pleasure
of blame

Fireman

i woke with a headache
my body felt used up
discarded food
trampled in the street

i could not have guessed
that i could work so long   so hard
engulfed in smoke and ashes
despair and bewilderment
tearing people's eyes

> it's not easy to
> find the truth
> on this table
> of politics and domination

Young Man

don't believe in much
don't know any god
but right now
i wanna believe in liberty
smoke blinding my eyes
sure hope she knows
i love her some plenty
she be the first person i ever loved
know now i shouldn't have had that affair
that was real wacked
love you fasure sherri

> *two wrongs don't make a right*
> then how to explain
> which terror
> precipitated which terror

West Indian Woman

lawd god look how me
come america fi betta me life
fi get weh from the violence
to come meet death this tuesday morning
what go happen to me four children
who gwane look afta dem
no place fi run

Security Guard

i told my idiotic boss
after the first tower exploded
we should evacuate

should've followed my gut feeling
screw being written up one more time
for not following orders
screw the pension
i've got a wife three children mortgage parents
damn these crazy folks
i just paid for our first cruise

every day when life is routine
reflect before
swearing at someone
for a slight infraction
don't neglect to tell
your children or mate
you love them
remember to smile
at the person walking right by you
stop complaining
be grateful

OUR OPPORTUNITY: KATRINA'S SURVIVORS

clarence henry's riff
ain't got no home
no place to roam
comes to me like
an ill-fated prophecy
when the levees broke
when the water rose
when they were left
stranded on rooftops
for more than three days

sidney bechet's reed
groans and whimpers
calling to all of us
on higher ground
mouths flapping endless complaints
fingers jabbing at who's to blame
what can we do
what must we do

satchmo's cornet
whips and thrashes
screams rising from the water
old with salt & the past
still in residence

satchmo's horn
blares what we already knew
poor equals neglected
a rusty nail infects

and the melody loops
seducing us into its rhythm
teasing us to dance
in broad daylight

KATRINA EXAMINED

if we hook our self-love
to the velocity
of the wind
how much love
would we have to spare?

if our words
fuelled our actions
to burst free
like the levees
would the need
to point blame
exist?

perhaps next week
or next year
our memories
will resurface
sunflowers
proud in summer
bloom

I AM KATRINA

(Inspired by Pablo Neruda's 'Ode to the Storm')

there is no shame
or remorse
about who i am
i have been maligned
called all kinds of names
have been portrayed
as wanton
merciless
but that is not who
i know myself to be

you see it was like this

i had been pleading
for you to stop
deforesting my trees
bombing my womb
thrashing my body

i had been stifling
my moans
tying up my locks
holding their affront

until
the weight
spilled from me
blowing my hair free
arms flailing
tears gushing from
my eyes
releasing all

WAVES OF RESILIENCE

the water has receded
but it remembers

the old woman pushing herself
in the wheelchair
until exhaustion and hunger
took over

the man in his car
key in engine with
his life's possessions
piled to the roof

the woman who
watched her children airlifted
and cried out loud
thank you lord
still hopeful
five days on the neighbour's roof
her ashy body bloated
fingers still clutching
the sliding house

all of them
and too many more
who got on buses
who couldn't get on buses
who were rescued by teenagers
only to be raped in the dome
those stranded
walking their way to
any kind of freedom
no moses with his god of magic
to hold back the levees

the water remembers
its hunger is ancient
for black flesh

now gentrification
a black-free mardi gras
a clintonesque harlem
a blueless filmore

erasing
and erasing
all the smudge

MISS BEAUTIFUL

she sits on the same bench
by the lake
every morning
reclining   elegant
in her disarray
as if she's waiting on someone
or just taking a rest

cracked heels
one leg stockinged
the other bare
lipstick smeared
like a clown's mouth

she does not speak or smile
she does not swear or glare
just listens to the music inside her head

on the ground
behind the bench
all her belongings
in four plastic shopping bags
she always finds a place to sleep
someone offers food   cigarettes
each day unfolds
and she perches
in shawl and make-up
like the lady she knows she is

perhaps tomorrow
the sun will light her heart
and jolt her memory
and she will find her way
back home

MISTER REJECTED

he had meant it
until death do we part
and was willing to do
whatever it took
to make her happy

but she stopped
loving him
and to drive her point home
brought another man
into their bedroom
then moved out
without
a forwarding address

he lost all reason
stumbled and slipped
can't chart his journey
to sleeping in the park
holding out a cup
too tired to do much else
her face her lovely chestnut face
still looking out of the eyes
of everyone from whom he begs

GAZING ON RWANDA

when elephants fight
the grass gets trampled

neither the hutu or the tutsis
gestate for twenty-two months
but their numbers have dwindled
in this thirty-years war
cousins decapitating cousins
neighbours butchering neighbours

i pretend blindness
but in my house
i walk without stumbling
even without seeing
my body remembers
where everything is
so what is this grudge
that wipes memory
clean of all the ordinary
everydayness
of things they shared
a broom a pinch of salt

this denial
of each other's humanity

DEVILS ON HORSEBACK

he rides her down
lunges from his horse
and in the open with others
watching and jeering
he rips off her hijab
tugs at her hair
laughs derisively
he is a janjaweed,
a muslim man
servant of mohammed
he knows she will be
banished forever
defiled   thrown out
he knows the terror
he precipitates
villages of women
silenced

he rips off her jilbab
and forces his way
between her thighs
gashes through vaginal muscles
this is more than rape

i heart chokes
cannot even moan
buried in the tissue
of its muscles
as i sister
is tossed on the ground
kicked   crumpled
too dazed to even whimper
before the next and the next
janjaweed thrusts into her
as damaging

as all the aerial bombardments
as all the sweltering villages set ablaze
as final as thousands of men slaughtered

i heart reach down on the
ground where ikraam lies
ikraam whose name means honour
i heart whispers to her
get up mother of three
get up wife who will never
be accepted as wife again
sister whose sister
already has been killed

i heart drones
i heart hums
i heart sings to
ikraam   asiya   haija

rise from the ground
i sisters
pick up your ripped hijab
and find refuge
for yourselves   your children

i heart knows
what this is about
i heart knows
that china   canada and
malaysia are stepping
over the carnage
drilling for oil

i heart knows
this is not a fable

ELEGY FOR IRAQ & THE USA

I

i am mother and daughter
sister and wife
cousin and aunt
godmother and grandmother
my womb has nursed life
i know pain
but their acid tears
burn through my understanding
their high-pitched voices
burst my eardrums

II

nazeeha raad was wife
her husband killed by a bomb
six months earlier
she lived in manawi pasha district
i met her cousin in egypt
she invited me to her home
served me tea and sweets

jamaal adams twenty-two years old
first time away from
louisville kentucky
i led a community poetry workshop
there a decade ago
his mother was a participant

najim ramadan
neighbour of abbas mahmoud
a quiet man who sold fruits at the market

benjamine edmundson twenty-two years old
the only child of a single mother
who worked two jobs most of her life
the last thing she told him
was to come back alive
so i will have someone
to pour me water when i get old

jabar abdul hafout
brother of mohammed
grandson of raad sakman
wanted to be a dentist one day
the bomb that exploded
tore off most of his face
roberto acklin oldest brother of three
somewhat quiet
worked well with his hands
made a mean spaghetti
ali latif coached football
his smile melted
the coldest of hearts
five years old tabarik
granddaughter of abbas ramadan
loved coloured ribbons and pomegranates

karrada franklin baghdad roswell anbar province
kifl hammond hawd baldwin baquba
wilson basar fort texas suweira orangeburg nasiriya
south carolina karbala savannah bayji
places and names forever fixed
in someone's memory

emily mackenzie   widad saed al-haidery
thaer saggban al-karkhi   vorn mack
khalid nasir   kenneth tyler
son of dead woman

boy under ten years old
two girls no more than six years old
five children under the age of twelve
son of living woman
son of father killed
son of living father
daughter of living woman
daughter of living children
wife adult woman
boy of ten
two girls about eight years old
father
son
son
son
members of our community

655,000 iraqis
4,091 americans	2 australians
176 britons	13 bulgarians
1 czech	7 danes
2 dutch	2 estonians
1 fijian	5 georgians
1 hungarian	33 italians
1 kazakh	1 korean
3 latvians	22 poles
3 romanians	5 salvadorians
4 slovaks	11 spaniards
2 thai	18 ukrainians

how many more
before we collapse under this weight
how much longer
before we shout enough
end this war

HUNTING

i hid
in the closet
as i often did as a girl

shut away
in the darkness
between the clothes

i stifled my breath
and listened
for my name

for a long long time
only silence
called out to me

i sneezed
       then
              i heard
                     a patter

it filled
my mouth

i knew
instantly
it was my name

ME

me the enslaved who ran
wah woman machete
ered me the one whose
bound whose womb
massa's blood me the
of
than
con-
case of
me-
help
more
and the
me
the
spirits
then is
many
me tired
me yes me
nice me who mind
is me same one

campung nanny
lime and vinegar
fusing the confused
i but the subject of
down second class
me god fi me pick-
me with the hunger
empty bancra
with chigger foot and yaws
yanga wheeling and
ride me who me not
who me who leggo
names me who
of the hus-
the same
me own

tegreg
whose
me the
me
self me
me the
nie
want-
bal-

to the hills me the talla-
aimed and blow deliv-
feet would not be
would never carry
gal goddaughter
mouth sourer
duppy spirit
not the objective
that refuse hand-
squatter the so
dem gwane have
ing to nyam me up
anced on me head
mouth me doing
turning until
me couldn't be
and is called by
between you and
tling and disrespect
one who know she
business and keep meself safe

ME

me the enslaved
who ran to the hills

me the tallawah woman
machete aimed and blow delivered
me the one whose feet
would not be bound
whose womb would never carry massa's blood

me the tegreg gal
goddaughter of campung nanny
whose mouth sourer than lime and vinegar

me the duppy spirit confusing the confused

me   not the objective case of i
but the subject of self

me that refuse hand-me-down
second class

me the squatter
the so-help-me-god
fi me picknie dem gwane have more

me with the hunger wanting to nyam

me up and the empty bancra balanced
on me head

me with chigger foot
and yaws mouth

me doing the yanga
wheeling and turning
until spirits ride me

who me   not me
couldn't be   then is who

me who leggo and is called
by many names

me who   between you and me
tired of the hustling and disrespect

me   yes me
the same one
who know she nice

me who mind me own business
and keep meself safe

is me
same one

NAMING

i insist they name their accomplices those who conspired to rob me of my name the name i have is not
the name my ancestors would have named me the name i have is a thief's name it is the name they
gave me and i am determined to retrieve my name to clear my name
to make a name for myself that cannot be abducted cannot
be traded cannot be sold i have gone by the rapist's name i
have used the kidnapper's name i am identified by the
buyer's name but these are not my names my father's name
has been blemished my mother's name is taken in vain and if i
am to make a name for myself i must know my name not a code
name or a brand name but my own name my people have been
given a bad name a name that has been trying to make them
disappear a pauper's name so they don't have a dollar to their name i
deserve a name that is worthy of my history i crave a name that
names my voyage the perils i have prevailed i refuse to be consid-
ered in name only i seek a performer's names i demand an overcomer's
name i insist on being well known by the name i name myself too
long i've assumed their name

II

the usurper is always dropping names barging into my house
hauling out my male relatives hollering open up in the name of the
law shooting before calling out halt in the name of the law but who
named the law the law the law has two names and i name one unequal
they drag me to the jail claim my name was mentioned in connection
with freedom that i was referred to by name that i am to give the names of
my compatriots many are named in connection with this
movement they say i give the exploiter's name my pen name my
stage name my summer name my pet name aliases aka nick names
my trader's name my buyer's christian name the boss's family
name the stockbroker's trade name the judge's forename
the journalist's byname and all the great names in
their history they demand to know my maiden name my
surname my first name what is your name they
hammer what is your last name i don't have a name
you can pronounce i say evenly bracing
myself for the fist i have a personal name that is my
armor it was sung to me at birth it was whispered
in my ears when i was raised up to the sun i was told to always
protect my good name my name is the self my name is the family my name is
the nation my name is the name i name myself

NAMING

i insist they name
their accomplices
      those who conspired
      to rob me of my name
the name i have is not
the name my ancestors
would have named me
      the name i have
      is a thief's name
          it is the name they gave me
and i am determined
to retrieve my name
to clear my name
to make a name for myself
that cannot be abducted
cannot be traded
cannot be sold

      i have gone by the rapist's name
      i have used the kidnapper's name
      i am identified by the buyer's name
      but these are not my names

my father's name has been blemished
my mother's name is taken in vain
and if i am to make a name for myself
i must know my name
      not a code name or a brand name
but my own name

      my people have been given
          a bad name   a name that has been trying
    to make them disappear
    a pauper's name so
      they don't have a dollar to their name

i deserve a name that is worthy of my history
      i crave a name that names my voyage
the perils prevailed over

      i refuse to be considered in name only
      i seek a performer's name
      i demand an overcomer's name
      i insist on being well known
by the name i name myself

too long i've assumed their name

II

the usurper is always dropping names
barging into my house
hauling out my male relatives
hollering   *open up in the name of the law*
shooting before calling out
halt in the name of the law

but who named the law the law
     the law has two names
     and i name one unjust
they drag me to the jail
claim my name was mentioned
     in connection with freedom
that i was referred to by name
that i am to give the names
of my compatriots

many are named
in connection with
this movement
they say

i give   the exploiter's name
          my pen name   my stage name
          my summer name   my pet name
          aliases aka   nicknames
          my trader's name   my buyer's christian name
          the boss's   family name
          the stockbroker's trade name
          the judge's   forename
          the journalist's   byname
          and all the great names in history

they demand to know my maiden name
my surname   my first name
                    what is your name
they hammer
                    what is your last name

i don't have a name
you can pronounce
i say evenly
bracing myself for the fist

i have a personal name
that is my armour
it was sung to me at birth
it was whispered in my ears
when i was raised up to the sun
i was told to always protect
        my good name

        my name is the self
        my name is the family
        my name is the nation
        my name is the name

i name myself

I NAME ME NAME

some call me
        black
                gal
sapphire

but
i
call myself
        i name me name

me this ebony
child woman

i'm not   someone's mistake
a relic   from history
        i name me name

it's a lie
they've been trying
        to shove down my throat
it's a lie
they've been trying
        to make me accept
        i name me name

my ancestors
were not merely slaves
my history is much older
than four hundred years

feel my breath
        cobwebs float
                from where i extend back
clay and wood

                become dust
                        swirl
                                into the day
                                        when touched
i name me name

before europeans
        landed on my ancestors' shores
cities fed and clothed
people
        armies built fortresses

i am not
a carbon copy
of my oppressor
i will not file
my nails
accept second-class
                citizenship
i name me name

I NAME ME 2

t
  u
    r
     n
    i
  n
g

20
rejected my father's name
refused a husband's name

i named
myself
to become
my own
self when i celebrated
30 years

t
  u
    r
     n
    i
  n
g

40 i searched for a new name
that eschewed conventions
opting to be recalcitrant
hair uncombed & naked

encircled now
by half a century
i am just woman
named and carefree

I NAME ME 3

i
     go
          alone
                    into
                         the
                              woods

seeking
the meaning
of who
i
am

i cannot identify
most of the sounds
i hear
eyes follow me
hidden among foliage

nestled beside
a rock
and a thorny bush

i recover
     a
          name
     to
          make
myself
     whole   holy

I NAME ME 4

like a hunter
tracks a lion

drinking from its
waterhole

sniffing its faeces
studying its trail

seduced by its
beastliness

i sniff and watch
drink blood from

the fountain
of my lineage

find my own face
in i heart's reflection

I NAME ME

found it
with meat and skin

an elixir
growing from the
pit of my arm

warrior & visionary
words & teaching

all i'm working
at being
all i've been
being

this is not a new name
this is not an old name

it is i name
the name i name iself

PART II

PROSE

SITTING BETWEEN MY MOTHER'S LEGS
(2005)

My fondest memory of myself as a little girl, up until I was eleven years old, is sitting between my mother's legs while she plaited my hair. Although sometimes I sat on the side of the bed, especially if it was Sunday morning getting ready for church, or sat on a chair, mostly I sat on a low stool between my mother's legs, my arms draped over her knees, often my head resting on the inside of one of her thighs while she oiled my scalp and plaited my hair. It is the most indelible and intimate memory I have of my mother, and I cherish this image.

Perhaps this is why my hair symbolizes intimacy and bonding whether with my mother or with my daughters who sat in the same manner when they were small. Perhaps that is why I have always, except for a brief stint between the age of thirteen and sixteen, worn my hair proud in its natural tight-curled texture. Perhaps I was destined to wear my hair natural because my great grandaunt Zilla, who was a consummate storyteller and lived in Johns Hall, Jamaica, always wore her hair natural in two or three plaits all her life, until 2003 when she died at the age of 102. Perhaps it was seeing all those market women, with their hair corn-rowed or plaited, rolling their cotta and placing it on their heads before hoisting up their baskets, and me thinking you needed to have strong hair to be able to carry such a heavy load with ease. Perhaps it was because at nine years old, when for the first time I left Jamaica with my mother and sister, to visit the World's Fair in New York, we met a group from Africa, and the women's hair was twisted and pointed in beautiful black spikes on their heads as they walked around in flowing bubas that made them appear as if they were floating. I distinctly remember that I asked my mother if I could wear my hair like them. Perhaps because I came of age during the Afro era, and discovered my beauty and sex appeal donning that style; perhaps because the hair of the first man I loved, my father, was natural and I loved how it felt when I rubbed his head; perhaps because I have always loved and been grateful that I am a woman of African descent with strong hair that defies all attempts to dominate or tame it, I have felt that natural hair means community, connectedness and sisterhood. Its care provides a necessary and essential time for women and girls to swap stories about life, and share important lessons that will help them over hurdles.

I have worn my hair plaited, sported an Afro for many years, flaunted braids, sometimes with extensions, and while I was in Ghana and Kenya had it twisted with thread, donned Miriam Makeba close-cropped, corn-rows, and now wear dreadlocks, the ultimate in freedom, versatility and beauty. My college-age daughter has groomed my hair this way from the beginning, when she had just entered high school. I have always loved the feel and texture of my thick hair. I love how it feels next to my face and back, I love how it feels when a man runs his fingers through it, I love its flow and resistance, I love its vine-like disposition. Most importantly, I love how it complements the features of my face and accentuates my cheekbones.

I no longer sit between my mother's legs, but the memories and lessons that came to me from that vantage point are treasures that I wear like the bangles on my arms that jingle with my every move. My kinky, stubborn hair, like other symbols of my culture and identity, represents my lineage and African ancestry that is important to me and forever enduring.

A BARREL OF LAUGHTER AND A BUCKET OF TEARS: ME AND MY SISTER
(1997)

My sister and I are a year and five months apart, and for almost twenty years we lived in the same house, were governed by the same rules, and shaped ourselves to be the women we are today. Although we live more than five hundred miles apart we are friends, though not as intimate as I would like us to be. Still, my sister Dawn is one person I know I can depend on, and I believe she knows she can depend on me.

My children love her, especially my daughter Shola who knows her better, being the oldest. Shola has been going to spend time with Dawn since she was less than a year old, staying a week or more at a time. One summer, my son, Jawara, then two years old, also went to stay with her. His first time away from his father and I; and I was sad that he didn't appear, from my daughter's report, to miss me like I missed him/them.

"Mummy, Jaja has forgotten about you guys." But, he was with my sister and I felt extremely fortunate that she would take my children for three weeks so I could get ready for my third child, due in a month.

My sister is also a mother. Her son is grown. I call him my first child, and love him dearly. She was a teenage mother. Just through high school at seventeen, she got pregnant, and kept her child, and abandoned her childhood dream to be a doctor. But Dawn went to college and got her B.S. in nursing, and is now a nurse administrator. She seems happy with her choices. I love my sister, trust her with my life, insisted that she accompany me when I had to have a Caesarean section with my daughter; I needed the pressure of her hand as I felt the knife slice through my flesh and they pulled at the baby. My sister was there for me, holding my hand, lending me her strength, reminding me of all the times while we were growing up of us being there together, sharing, taking care of and covering for each other, fighting to protect one another. When my daughter was born she became Aunty-Mother.

There is a picture of my sister and I when we she was seven and a half and I was six. We have on yellow taffeta nylon dresses with long streamers tied at the back, and we each have two ribbons in our hair, yellow, to match our dresses. Our hair is plaited in three, the way I used to like Mummy to do it. We're standing under a great tree, looking directly into the camera. We are holding hands, smiling. Nothing unusual about the picture; it could be of any two sisters, except it isn't. It is my sister and I. I imagine I see what no one else will see from looking at the photograph. I see my sister and I in love with each other, itching to run off some place and play without the scrutiny of others, or the restrictions of our delicate, pretty dresses.

I remember, and long for the days when my sister's tears were mine and mine were hers, when we laughed at the same thoughts, romped like month-old cubs and conspired like brazen outlaws ready to rob a train. Then we were closest, with no secrets between us; then we lived for each other, and wanted no one else; then we were carefree children and we, or at least I, never dreamed those days would become only a memory.

My sister and I didn't always agree; we fought like all siblings do. I remember clearly, shortly after my mother left our father and took us from the home they shared, the fight my sister and I had. I believe it was our first fight. Dawn was five and I was not yet four. Mummy gave Dawn, as the older, a shiny red apple to share between us. I so wanted to share the apple, but Dawn refused. After failed attempts to get the apple from her, scrambling over the bed, I sunk my teeth into her stomach, just below her navel, and bit with all my might. She screamed, the apple fell on the floor and I never got any. I never meant to hurt her.

I loved my sister, loved her to death; we were pals. We played hopscotch, school, London Bridge, ring-around-the-roses; we walked hand around the waist across the cricket field to get cow's milk in the morning, the wet dew tickling our soles because we kicked off our shoes to enjoy the feel of the grass. Sometimes we laid in the tall grass and drank unscaled raw cow's milk, and spied on adults going about their business. Mummy taught us to respect others, and we grew up in a Jamaican community in which everyone greeted each other, no matter the relationship, or whether or not you knew the person. Children were especially mindful to greet elders, and heed their words. My sister and I never transgressed this rule. But one morning, after my sister and I returned from fetching the milk, Mummy spanked us because a malicious spinster beat us home and told her that we were misbehaving in the streets, had failed to greet her and Duggie, the caretaker, and were generally rude. Mummy hit us on our bottoms, fuming that she raised us with manners, insisting that grownups didn't lie on children. Dawn and I cried, taking refuge under the large mahogany dining table, pledging our hate for the childless hag, tears mingling with snot as we continued to cry long after the hurt had subsided, but feeling the need to make the moment last, our anger and grief a bond to which we clung.

That afternoon, after the stain of tears had gone from our cheeks, and our spirits had again soared from play, Mummy returned from work and apologized to us. She learned that some grownups do lie about children, and promised never to spank us again without first listening to our side of the story. We never found out why that woman lied on us, but we learned later that many children got spanked because of her wagging tongue.

Dawn and I had lots of fun. We climbed trees: guava, tamarind, ackee, mango. Neither of us learned to climb the coconut tree, although I tried many times, watching those men who saddled up with such ease and grace, rope tied around their ankles to aid them in their ascent to rescue the sweet jelly coconuts from the crown of the tree. Still Dawn and I were champion tree climbers, and few boys in the neighbourhood could match our speed or agility. Because I was small, often called Tiny or Bird, I went to the peak of all trees, yet never fell nor broke my arm showing off, as Michael, Dennis and Beverly did on different occasions. Once I did slip in my scamper down our mango tree when I came face to face with a duppy lizard, changing its colour from green to gray to brown. After that I never climbed that mango tree again, relying on Dawn to be generous with the mangoes, and she always was, which was especially kind because Bombay mangoes were a favourite among all of us.

Best of all were those times when Dawn and I were accomplices and we ganged together our force to beat up those children, mostly boys, in the neighbourhood, who often teased and picked on us. We had a field day with Keithy, who used to tease Dawn because he liked her, and had spread a rumour throughout the neighbourhood that she was his girlfriend. We got our older brother to string Keithy up by the wrists on a tree as people often did to thieves they caught, then we used tamarind switches, which were known for stinging the skin, to flog him. Tears flowed like a hose from his eyes; he hollered for his brothers, the seat of his crotch wet, wailing like a dog hit by a car. Keithy never looked at us too closely after that. In fact, for a long time we made him ask permission just to look at us or be in our company. He was expected to cross the street whenever he saw us approaching. My sister and I enjoyed that victory, and it served as a warning to others to be cautious; the Palmer girls were known to be fighters.

Dawn and I were daring, sometimes defying rules Mummy set for us. Often, when she was at work, and we were left with the helpers, we would sneak off to swim naked in the canal, hunt birds in the thick bushes, walk for miles to the alligator pond, go fishing way down the river, or just run around and get scratches and lost in the cane-fields or some other daring activity that we children in the neighbourhood contrived for adventure. I was usually the instigator of our trips, hating to stay home and read or play with dolls. But Dawn enjoyed them just as much, except for that one time we went to the alligator pond, and I tried to jump across the narrow part of the swamp like the older boys, and fell and probably would have slid into the pond, food for the hungry alligators, if some of the older boys had not been alert, and quickly pulled me up from the banking. In the process I lost my brand new red shoes that Mummy had bought only the Saturday before. I could feel my heart in my throat, and Dawn and I sat on the banking looking down at the alligators, her arms around me. Everyone was quiet. None of us were really allowed to go to the alligator pond. What if I had fallen in? We all stood and sat around for several minutes, then without anyone saying anything we all left, branching off on the different paths to our homes once we got to the main road. But as I approached our house, one foot a shoe missing, I wished I had fallen in and the alligators had eaten me. How would I explain to Mummy what I was doing at the alligator pond, or even why I was wearing my new shoes? As Dawn and I took our afternoon bathe, to be clean when Mummy came home from work, we put our heads together and came up with a plan. We blamed Frisky, a fluffy brown puppy we had recently got, who was in the habit of chewing on shoes; on more than one occasion he had taken away a shoe and hidden it in the bushes at the back of our yard. Frisky took the blame, I got a new pair of shoes, and the alligators didn't even get to have me for lunch. I believe that was the last time we went to the alligator pond, except once returning from school, when Harrison, the school bus driver, took us to another pond on the estate where they were skinning an alligator. All of us children got royal chocolate fudges as we watched the men sever the skin from the body. I remember feeling some kind of victory over the alligator. And whenever I went to the club house where they hung that alligator's skin, I felt great satisfaction that his relatives hadn't eaten me.

There were other frightful moments, especially when it seemed my sister turned on me. I was scared of lizards, even the tiny polly lizards that hid in corners or under window sills, but my sister had no such fear. Often, she and some of the older boys ganged up against a few other girls and I. They caught lizards in the leaves of coconut boughs, and chased us. I would run screaming, then cower, petrified near the sunflower patch growing by our bedroom window. If Mummy was home I would run and crouch at her feet, or if Beatrice, our maid, was around, I would fly into her ample arms, and she would scold my sister and tell her to stop teasing me. I didn't like my sister on such occasions, not so much because she chased me, but because she joined forces with others against me. My fears of lizards increased as they seemed to be everywhere, even in the sunflower patch that I so loved, kneeling as I did every morning to open my bedroom window to let their marmalade fragrance float into our room. That was my habit until I discovered that lizards liked sunflowers too. Then my phobia spread like love-bush.

Dawn and I shared a bedroom, and although we had separate beds we often slept together. However, when I really needed to feel safe, I would try to persuade my mother to come and sleep with me, even though I was probably nine or so at this time. A gigantic croaking lizard took up residence in our room, behind the Grundig stereo box on the top of our closet. I refused to sleep in my bed which was nearest to the closet. After allowing me to sleep with her for a few nights, Dawn declined my continuing request to share her bed because she said I kicked too much, and always flung my leg over her. I was adamant about not sleeping in my bed; Dawn offered no shelter. Mummy said I had to get over this fear of lizards as they were everywhere, which they were, and quite harmless, fearing me probably more than I feared them. I didn't buy that line, so took my pillow and sheet and decided to make my bed in the bath tub since that was the only place in the house I had not so far seen any lizards. Mummy said I was being silly, and insisted that I return to my bed. I told her the croaking lizard that had been nesting in the crevice of the ceiling was laughing at me. Mummy got a broom and drove the lizard away, so I went to lie down.

The lights were turned off, and I covered my head. But the night was hot, and besides I couldn't resist looking up at the spot where the croaking lizard had been, and there it was again, looking like a rusty pipe staring at me, mocking me, croaking, calling its mate. I jumped up screaming, tearing at my clothes, believing that it had jumped on me and got in my nightie. Dawn wanted to sleep and was annoyed at my nightmare. How could she be so insensitive? Mummy came and put me back in bed. There was no lizard, she said. They didn't understand. My sister didn't care for me. I was silent in my fear, the gigantic croaking lizard sounding like an army marching band while my sister slept soundly. How could she? How could she be so separate, not feel or share my fear? I felt deserted, deprived of my best friend, my sister, my idol.

There were some fears my sister and I shared – as when Gem, who was like an adopted sister, found some white mice nesting in our galoshes during the wet season, and chased us out into the rain, over into Mrs. Kelly's yard, into the streets, laughing as she chased us over to the club house, around the cricket field, threatening to throw the mice on us. Dawn was hollering and, though I did not really care, because my sister feared those little pink creatures I hollered too. I was afraid because she was afraid and I wanted to share everything with her; I wanted us to be inseparable.

Simple pleasures. Dawn and I often hugged and laughed as we

did a fiddler's jig. At night we would lie at opposite ends of the bed and play 'Mosquito Jump into Hot Callalloo', our feet pedalling to the jingle. We pillow fought, beating the pillows open, feathers flying all over, before landing on our wooden floor, like the snow which we could never imagine. But once our laughter turned to tears when I held the pillow in my teeth. Dawn tugged so hard that she pulled loose one of my teeth. Blood was everywhere. We were both so surprised and frightened upon seeing the blood that we hollered for Mummy. That night my sister rubbed my back until I fell asleep.

I will always remember that Saturday morning when I became a Woman. At first, even though I knew about menses, I was frightened, but my mother consoled me, and told me to get the book from my sister on menstruation, the same book Dawn had gotten a year-and-a-half earlier. I can still feel the silence that morning as Dawn and I rocked in our separate chairs on the veranda; we shared each other's knowledge and secret of womanhood, and for a moment, just for a few seconds, I was angry at my sister when it occurred to me that she had kept her secret from me for over a year. Then I was happy again, happy that we both were Women, as Mummy said, and we were so close, so close in our womanliness. But then something happened. I still wanted to play and romp wild; tomboy, my mother and others called me. My sister was becoming a little lady, and before I knew what was happening she raced ahead, and left me behind, left me feeling more abandoned than I had ever felt before.

I was so happy in my sister's presence, and thought she was the brightest person there was. She was going to be a doctor and cure my nosebleeds rather than rely on placing a cold metal key on my forehead. I was going to be a lawyer since everyone agreed I was a chatterbox, and often spoke for both of us. We shared everything, or so I thought. I loved it that Mummy dressed us alike, and I wanted us to always remain together, identical, attached. So, I redoubled my efforts to be like my sister, though not enjoying the notion of being a lady, but not willing to walk behind, or separate from her.

I was, for example, really disturbed by our Anglican religion, and believed the whole thing somewhat hypocritical, too critical of enjoyment, and with too much emphasis on sin and repentance. Yet still I made Confirmation because the previous year Dawn had gone through the ritual. I wanted us to drink of the same blood and eat of the same flesh.

I took to praying earnestly to God, not for myself, but for my sister, and I was sure my wishes would be granted. But she didn't pass all her 'O' levels. So I ceased praying and cursed the Father, the Son and the Holy Ghost – I broke off communion with them, something which I felt Dawn had done with me lately, always preferring to hang out with the girls at her high school, them giggling and whispering and making references to boys, and other things which I just didn't get. I decided it was time to go my own way. . . My sister was sixteen and I was fourteen and a half.

We migrated to New York a year and a half later so we could attend college. I hated leaving home, resented leaving my friends, the sun, the beach, the familiar; hated the subway with its constant booming noises; hated living in an apartment for the first time, no big back yard with trees to climb, lean against, a place to get away from others, a place to think; hated the cold, never being able to get warm; hated the hostility, the indifference, no one greeting you on the streets, being nameless, no one knowing you or even caring that I was "Miss Palmer daughter that you know; see how she favour her"; I hated being without my sister for six months because she was left behind to retake those 'O' levels – which she passed. But when she arrived she also discovered that she was pregnant. What to do? How to break the news to Mummy? Fear! Shame. Uncertainty; sitting on the bed that afternoon, the news hung between us. Tears streaming down our cheeks, my arms around my sister, I tried to console her, telling her it would be okay; college could be postponed for a year, Mummy would understand. That day we touched. We were as close as we ever were. I shared her pain and confusion. We were sisters again, under the mahogany table, the hurt and anger long since dissipated, but not wanting to give up the moment, the sharing of common tears.

Then, when her son, my nephew was born, I declared that he was my son, too. I wanted him to call me Mother as he did her, believing that I too was his mother, although he knew that I was only his aunt. I felt so close to her, to him and we raised him together. I remember that Sunday morning when he fell and busted his head on the table. We wrapped him in towels and I held him in my arms as my sister drove at a maddened pace to the doctor. He was two years old then. I was just beginning my sophomore year. She was a freshman, working part time at the telephone company, all of us – she, Mummy and I – helping to raise her son.

My sister and I are not as close any more and that saddens me. We talk at least once a week on the phone. We know we can depend on each other for anything, but I no longer know her fears, or pains or disappointments, and I am sure she doesn't know mine. I want us to know each other like we used to, I want us to talk like we used to, not only about our relatives and the things they are and are not doing, but about us; I want us to shed tears, but I know that this is probably a dream – like my rude awakening when I discovered how difficult love is even under the best of circumstances. It seemed so simple when we were in ribbons – our love was a ball that we tossed in the air and always caught. But now we are women with families and we no longer reside under the same roof, nor even in the same city. But my children love her, and will not go for long without asking to visit Aunty and for that I am happy.

I wonder sometimes whether she, too, occasionally reflects and longs for yesterdays. Remembers those times when we wore identical clothes, and people mistook us for twins. We pretended we were. I wanted us to be twins, that's why I was so possessive, wanting us to go through every phase together. I wanted to defy nature, but I couldn't and that's when she started to branch off. I hated her friends for taking her away from me. Now, after all these years I am beginning to understand why I abhor anyone who interferes with close relationships I form; it is because I am seeking that closeness I shared with Dawn, and I can't find it, not anywhere, not with anyone, because no one is able to understand the depth of my craving: all those times I thought she didn't love me because we disagreed; all those times I withdrew into myself like a snake, hiding from her in the closet, in a box, or by a desolate tree because she didn't believe in what I did. All those times. Now we seem so different, though my husband says in some ways we're not. I find it hard to convince myself that we grew up under the same roof, under the same set of rules for twenty years. I am the horn of a bull, and she the nose of a puppy. She doesn't taste my tears any more; I don't see her sorrows. I know she is not very happy without me, but she doesn't know it. I know that I am not very happy without her. Dawn, say yes, our tears were a single trail of love. Say yes, our laughter was a flock of kiss-kee-dees on the hill and we were bursting with happiness like a flamboyant tree blooming red in July. We did enjoy each other, didn't we? Swinging ourselves to the ground, licking out too many cake bowls, racing in the evening to see who would kiss Mummy first when she returned from work. All those things we did without thinking of tomorrow, which is today.

Now we are two women, alike, yet alone. Sometimes we are still so close, talking on the telephone or reminiscing about some relative, our laughter exploding like a fuse set to a barrel of gunpowder. Other times, we're so distant, even when visiting each other, that I feel I must keep to myself the buckets of tears that want to spill out.

I BECAME THE STORIES MY MOTHER TOLD ABOUT ME
(2005)

"She wasn't even three years old yet, you know, when she climbed the guava tree and I thought she would fall and die. Ah telling you her father and I didn't even see when she left the veranda, where we were entertaining friends, to go outside and climb the tree. To this day, we don't know how she was able to climb so far. My dear, my heart was in my mouth as I tried to coax her down, while her father climbed up to as far as he could without the limbs breaking under him. 'Come down, baby,' I said softly, while she hung above, smiling down at us. Finally she crept down a little way, and her father positioned himself, his back leaning against the trunk of the tree, while our friends stood under the tree, arms spread, ready to catch her if she should slip. But her daddy caught her and climbed down with her. Ah tell you I was so relieved all I could do was laugh," my mother ends, laughing loudly, as is her habit. One of the visitors, whose name and face I don't remember, grabs hold of my hand and says, "So is so you womanish from you was baby." I nod my head, knowing he is not really expecting a reply, or that whatever I say will be used as further evidence of my self-willed, womanish ways, which I am always being told about.

My mother is a storyteller, at least this is how I think of her. She has a story to suit every occasion, but mostly it seemed she had a story about me that she felt compelled to share with relatives, friends and even strangers. I had heard the above story before, countless times. I think it must have been one of my mother's favourites, which is why she kept telling it every opportunity she got. I was her favourite character, just as my favourite character is Anansi with his trickster ways. Perhaps there's a connection: we're both small and we both know how to get out of tight situations. Still, I wished my mother hadn't felt the need to tell almost everyone a story about me. Soon she had her sisters and other relatives making up stories about me too and telling them to others. Even now, everywhere I go, I am greeted by such stories.

Very early, I am not sure how old I was, I was dubbed Miss Madam or Mother-Pepper by my aunts and other women close to the family. I cannot recall what, if any, specific action spawned that title, except my mother says I was always ready with a rejoinder, regardless of what anyone said, even in an era when the maxim was, "Children should be seen and not heard". I did not abide by that aphorism, not because I was deliberately recalcitrant, but mainly because there was so much I wanted to understand and things I felt obliged to test out for myself. Consequently, quite often people would say when referring to me, "Miss Palmer, you must have given that one chicken bottom to eat why she chat so much." Jamaicans believe that eating that part of the chicken leads to diarrhoea of the mouth. So an aunt would look towards me and say offhandedly, "That one has more stories than river have water or yam have starch, and she have de other children under manners like headmistress with cane. De poor little ones dem so afraid of her that even if their mothers call, they will not answer or get up to leave unless de Miss Madam gives them permission. Miss Madam has dem under control." This would be my mother's cue to launch into a specific incident she witnessed, when I was the teacher and playing school with the other children in the neighbourhood, to give more meat to her sisters' comments, how I was a firm disciplinarian, or maybe that I did not take to anyone trying to boss me around.

"Did I tell you about the time that she pulled out that little white boy's hair and pushed him in the back?" My mother pauses and looks around, making sure she has everyone's full attention. Her face is expressive, eyes dancing off the faces of those gathered, then on mine, making sure that I, too, am listening. Certain of undivided attention, my mother clears her throat, then continues. "I think it was a Wednesday afternoon, I was at the office working, when I looked up to see Mr. Harrison, the school bus driver. 'Good afternoon Miss Palmer,' he said tipping his hat. 'Good afternoon, Mr. Harrison,' I replied, feeling somewhat concerned, wondering why he was here to see me. 'Is everything okay Mr. Harrison?' He nodded yes, and then gave a shy smile. 'Well ma'am, I am here to ask you not to spank you little one, if you get any complaint against her. Between you and me ma'am, she do we well this afternoon.' By now I was at the edge of my chair," my mother intones, her face like an African funeral mask. "I couldn't imagine what Opal could have done on the school-bus to warrant Mr. Harrison coming to see me and interceding on her behalf. I hastily asked, 'What happen Harrison? What happened on the bus today?' Harrison took out a plaid handkerchief and mopped his brow, then he twisted the brim of his hat between his hands. 'Well you know, ma'am, dat we have dis new little boy from England on de bus. Well him don't listen, and him bother all de children, but as him is manger son, me don't say too much to him. Even though him just come, him feel him can sit anywhere him like and no one else matter. Well you know your girls sit upfront with me. Well today me pick him up first and him jump in the front of the Land Rover. Me tell him seh is Miss Palmer's daughters' seat up front, but him slam the door and seh to me, just drive, you're not in charge here. Imagine dat, Miss Palmer, dis little white boy come and disrespect a big man like me, but since him is de big manager son, me don't say anything. Well me go pick up your girls. The big one go in the back, but little Opal stand outside and tell him to move cause him in her seat. Him seh him nah move. Me tell her to come cause we blocking traffic. She get in the back and slam de door. She sit down right behind him. Same way dem start fi argue and him seh to her, "Just you shut up, you black girl because I'm in charge." Well who tell him fi seh that? Little Opal jump up and pull him blond hair and shout, "How you can be in charge and you just come to Jamaica and you red like shrimp and you chat like marble in you mouth. Get up out ah me seat or me gwane pull out all you hair." Miss Palmer, a tell you, by now the boy screaming so loud me have to pull off the road. Me tell little Opal fi let go of him hair, but she seh not until him move. By now him a cry, eye-water and snot running down, wetting him shirt. Little Opal drag him over the back and she and her sister take them seat and we drive home, him a sniffle all de way. Me say, Miss Palmer, is de quietest the school bus ever been. When me drop off de little boy, him run out de bus crying, so me know him a go tell him mama, so me just want you fi know how it go. De boy rude and no have no manners. Him think him can just talk to people anyway. Your daughters dem neva talk to me like de way dis fresh boy talk to me. So even though she shouldn't pull out him hair, him did deserve it. Ah just want you to know cause ah know him mama gwane call and complain.' 'Thank you, Mr. Harrison,' I said, anxious to get home to hear it from the girls. But before I left the office, Mrs. Coolthon, Dennis, the boy in question mom, called me on the phone hot-hot. I had was to tell her to calm down, that I am not in the habit of getting in the middle of children's quarrel and fight, and that there are always two sides to every story. I told her I had it from good source that Dennis insulted my daughters, that he had been behaving rather badly on the bus, and that he took their seats and refused to get up. Well, she butt in, he has a bald spot from where my unruly daughter pulled out his hair. I got hot then and had to put her in her place, nicely of course, and told her that my daughter was certainly no more unruly than her son, and she should be careful of how she throw words at other people's children. Furthermore, I added, your son needs to understand that this is not England, but Jamaica, and children are expected to respect all adults, and when he is on the school bus Mr. Harrison is in charge, and he needs to listen to and respect him. Ah tell you, by the time I was done dressing her down, she apologized to me and said she would be sure to make Dennis apologize to my daughters, which he did, and he and Opal fast became good friends and would go trekking through the woods together. My dear, I am telling you, Opal is not to be messed with." My mother ends and nods in my direction as if to salute me. I nod and smile in return.

This is actually one of my favourite stories that my mother tells about me. I like who I am being in this story, I like that I will not allow anyone to displace me, that I am prepared to take up for myself. However, no matter how hard I try to bring to mind what I was thinking and feeling as I pulled out Dennis's hair and demanded that he relinquish my seat, I cannot. Was I enraged? Did I feel the slightest fear that my actions would get me in trouble, even spanked? I wish my mother knew those details and added them to the story, then I would have a fuller picture of what motivates me emotionally. Nonetheless, I *was* scolded for pulling out Dennis's hair and warned about my *tegereg* behaviour. But Mummy never includes her disciplining part when she tells the story. I never try to tell these stories about myself because I don't really think they belong to me; they are my mother's stories that she shares with relatives and friends. It seems my entire life is a story that she eagerly shares.

By the time I was eight years old, I was well accustomed to being called Weeny, Bird, Little Bit, but I, of course, could only see myself as myself and so was always surprised when people commented about how tiny I was. Friends came to visit; they would declare, "What a way she fine and tiny." I suspect my mother felt as if her parenting method was being judged. She often tried to cajole, then force me to eat to fatten me up so others wouldn't remark about how small I was.

My mother responds to her visitors, "My dear, determined." I hear a story fermenting so stand with one hand on my hip, hoping my mother will not reel off another story about me, but she sends me to bring juice for the guests. I walk to the kitchen reluctantly, not wanting to miss the grownups' talk, but also relieved that I don't have to suffer through the story. As I re-enter the living-room, arms weighed down with a tray bearing three tall glasses of passionfruit juice, I hear my mother launch into a familiar story, and I want to be off, far away, under a tree so I don't have to hear it again, but I know I have to stay until dismissed. I chew on my lip, and pretend to listen as if I am hearing this story for the first time. "My dear, that one there is not afraid of anyone." My mother pulls me to her, and I hear the music, but also the pride in her voice. "I remember this time when she was just three years old and we went to visit my sister and her husband, Ronald. Well Ronald had a cousin who was a very big man, about 6' 2" and strapping, and he liked to tease and I think the cousin thought he would scare her, so he said, 'Look how tiny you are, and look how big I am, I could just chop you up.' Well she was standing right next to him. She put her hands on hips, looked him up and down and said, 'Before you chop me up, me would kick you and run.' And so saying she kicked him on his shin and sprinted away. Well he was so taken aback, all he could do was laugh. Then he said to me, 'Miss Catherine, you don't need to worry about that one, she can take care of herself.'" My mother cackles at her own telling and the guests join her in laughter. I am not amused, cannot see the joke in it. I feel all their eyes on me. My mother looks at me, as if seeking confirmation or maybe thinking I might add other details, but I look off, acting as if I am not even there, as if they are not talking about me.

Although I had heard my mother tell that story several times, always it seems to me with a great deal of bravado, I literally do not remember the incident, but always as she tells it, as she is telling it, I picture myself through her eyes, doing and saying what she said I said and did. Initially the incident was not fixed in my memory. However, after being forced to sit through many retellings, it is like a moving picture in my own head, and that is how it remains, with my mother as narrator, like a hypnotist.

I used to detest when relatives or friends came to visit and my mother got on her soapbox and retold, for the umpteenth time, a story about something I had done that she thought, in hindsight, was funny. However, to hear her tell it, it was usually not funny when it was happening, so why she chose to keep retelling it baffled and embarrassed me.

What I found even more distressing was my mother's insistence that I was present as she told the story. I felt as though I was being asked to stand and undress in front of strangers while they scrutinized my body, or even more aggravating, while thy laughed over something that I had allegedly done that I could not recall. They often stared at me closely to see if there was still any evidence of the story, as if it had just happened, rather than years ago, when I was too young to remember. I can still feel their eyes on me, see their abandoned laughter, and even hear their sighs, and aaahms at various stages of the story, and how they inserted commentary as my mother went on. How I hated those moments!

This particular afternoon my mother sits with friends on the front veranda, and although I am being very quiet, trying to be invisible so I could eavesdrop on their conversation (a favourite pastime of mine), I am spotted behind the chair where I sit, knees pulled to my chest, arms wrapped around my legs. (I don't recall what jarred this story, maybe the fact that I had just wandered off again, gone all day, roaming about enjoying my own company, and my mother wanted to illustrate that her mind was at ease, confident as she was in my independent capability.)

"I will never forget this afternoon," my mother begins, leaning forward in her chair, excitement evident in her voice, "I was inside crocheting, and the maid ran and called me; she said to look through the kitchen window. There was Opal, her sister to her back, with a long stick in her hand that she was swinging around with force, aiming it at the group of children who had them surrounded. Opal was taunting them: 'Tease me again and see if ah don't knock yu wid me stick.' She actually hit a few of the children, all of whom were older than her. But I will tell you this, that was the last day they teased her, and she could always play, even with the older children because she proved that she could and would defend herself, regardless of who."

I cover my face and smile behind my hand. My mother shoos me to go and play. I run off, but turn back chanting, "Ah go knock you wid me stick, Ah go knock you wid me stick."

At some point, my mother gave up on trying to fatten me, a hopeless endeavour (I almost never finished any meal, and really only enjoyed fruit), and switched instead into trying to make me a "lady" (another hopeless endeavour, but she didn't know it at the time), which in her mind meant I did not run wild and play police and thief or cricket with the boys, didn't fight, even in self-defence, didn't wander off and swim naked or go to the alligator pond with the boys, didn't shout at the top of my lungs, or argue ferociously to have my way. I was to be demure and sweet, rather than boisterous and self-possessed. I chose the latter as it suited my natural disposition. Outwardly, I humoured her, but privately thought a mad duppy had taken over her head. I sneaked off and continued in my tomboyish behaviour, and the boys in the neighbourhood knew not to mess with me, or try to exclude me from their games or I would make their lives miserable.

A new boy moved into our community and tried to rile me up by messing with one of my dogs. All week he and I had been back and forth, me beating him three times straight in arm-wrestling, and the last straw was when I won his favourite green-eyed marble on Saturday. The following afternoon when he saw me at Sunday school in my dress and lace socks, he naively thought he had the upper hand.

My mother doesn't know this back story, but as we sit for Sunday dinner, months later, with guests, she chimes: "Did I ever tell you about the time Opal fought at church? I had was to scold her sternly, even though I was secretly amused. Here it is a Sunday afternoon, I am home relaxing, she and her sister went to Sunday school, and one of my neighbours barge into my house, dragging her son to show me his bloody nose, shirt still fresh with blood, that she claimed Opal did, unprovoked. Now mind you, her son Michael, at twelve, is two years older than Opal, and at least a head taller. Still I was shocked that she would be fighting, of all places in church, when I have been telling her that she is too old to be carrying on like that, and it is not ladylike behaviour. She hadn't come home yet, so I got up and sat on the veranda so I would see her as soon as she came home. Well my dear, even before she walked though the gate, I knew she had been in a scuffle as one braid was all undone, her dress was ripped at the waist, and on close inspection, she had a scratch on her face. I was so angry, I didn't even wait to find out what happened. I shouted at her, 'Did I send you to church to fight?' Her sister came to her defence. 'Mummy, is Michael start it first.' I sighed and sat on the chair. 'Opal, why you must bloody the boy's nose?' I asked her."

And at this point I took over the story.

"All week Michael want to fight me," I said, "but I tell him I not fighting no more; and he said, 'I hear dat you think you is bad girl, but bet you, you don't bad like me.' I just walk away from him and said, 'Is who you? Why I should care what you think,' and kiss my teeth at him. Well during Sunday school when I trying to pay attention, he's mumbling under his breath and almost gets me in trouble, but I don't say anything to him. But when Sunday school was over, Brownie was waiting for me under the tree, and as soon as I whistle to Brownie, Michael start. 'Look how you dog ugly, bet you ah stone him.' And right way he picks up some small pebbles and toss them as Brownie. Ah say to him, 'Michael leave me dog!' but him don't stop. Me and Brownie walk away, and he follows us, picks up more pebbles and toss at Brownie. One hit Brownie on his hind leg and he whimpers, then barks. Ah turn around and ah say to Michael, 'You better not throw any more stones at me dog. Poor Brownie can't defend himself,' but

Michael don't listen. Him get a handful of pebbles and start tossing them. So I run up to him, to get the pebbles from his hand and he push me. I push him back, and he grabs a hold of my plait. I kick him, and by now Brownie is barking and Ah thinking Brownie gwane bite Michael, so I make to thump Michael and my fist connect with his nose, and same time it start to bleed and he begin to cry like a baby and run off crying that him gwane tell his mother. Is him start it first and I just trying to make sure him didn't hurt Brownie," I end.

My mother looks over at me. All eight pairs of eyes around the dinner table stare at me. My mother's best friend, Aunt Nora, breaks the mood,

"Cathy, Ah don't know what you go do with her. She bad fah true."

Her son, who is also twelve, looks at me and challenges, "No ten-year-old girl can bust my nose!"

His mother gives him a stern look and says, "Is fight you want to start at Aunt Cathy's dinner table this afternoon. Don't worry about Opal busting your nose, I will do it for you if you don't mind you own business."

"Junior darling," my mother says to Junior to soften his mother's reprimand, "Opal is a tegereg from long time. I wouldn't take her on if I were you." Then my mother looks over to me and says, "Eat your food."

I pick out the peas from the rice and put a forkful of rice in my mouth. I chew slowly, and when I think my mother and Aunt Nora are too engrossed in conversation to see me, I stick my tongue out at Junior.

Long after this dinner, my mother continues to tell these and other stories until I don't listen any more. But when I close my eyes and lie quiet, I often hear her voice and I see myself through her eyes. Yet, strangely, the stories give me an opportunity to look in on a girl who looks like me, but isn't me, rather is the girl becoming me. I realize now that my mother, whether consciously or unconsciously, by telling and retelling those stories about my various antics, was allowing me to see certain character traits, as well as she was imprinting them on my memory. Through her storytelling, I fortified important character strengths that have seen me through the years. Now I tell my children stories about themselves, hoping they too will glean important intuitive traits about themselves that will help them on the path of life that they must tread.

Thank you, Mummy, for treasuring my stories and giving them back to me as ladders with which I keep scaling fences.

MOVING: FOUR MOVEMENTS TO A TREE
(2006)

1. Guava Tree

My mother, sister and I are crowded in the front of the truck with the driver, bags at our feet, the back of the truck piled with furniture and boxes. Before the truck glides out of the driveway I see my father sitting on the veranda of our home; he seems so still I fear he might be dead. As the truck rolls out, I notice the tears streaming down my mother's face. I wrap my arms around her neck as she wipes them away. The truck idles. I glance again and know that Daddy is breathing, can see his chest rise and fall. I wave goodbye to Daddy, but he does not wave back. I kneel on the seat, wanting to make sure Daddy sees me waving at him. Bye Daddy, I swallow as the truck pulls out the driveway, horn blaring, before it turns left, away from the only home I had known, away from that life shared with Mummy and Daddy, my sister and I and sometimes my two older half-brothers on Daddy's side.

I don't remember the drive, whether it was long, whether Mummy packed a snack or whether there were people on the road. What freezes in my mind like a photograph is: us in the truck, and Daddy on the veranda, pretending he doesn't see us, acting as if we don't exist. No matter how much I try to erase that image, it is rooted in the very core of my being. Perhaps it is all the more indelible because until the day we moved neither my mother nor my father said they were breaking up, or that we were moving, or where to or why. One minute I was playing and the next minute I was told to get my doll because we were leaving. I know I didn't think "leaving" meant it was going to be permanent. I know, at the time, I didn't understand that this would be a life-altering experience. I know I didn't think that I was not going to return or have the chance to say goodbye to my friends. I know I didn't understand why all of our furniture was in the back of the truck. I know I didn't understand why Daddy wasn't coming with us. I know I did not yet know what moving meant.

I was four and half years old on that first move, and I often wonder how that little girl processed that move, where I folded and hid my pain, how it has impacted on my sense of impermanence and my wariness over trust; how it shaped my psyche, influenced my attitudes to men, marriage and physical place? I know the little girl in me still wants to have my mother and father sit me down and tell me they are breaking up, and that Mummy got a job somewhere else so she is taking my sister and I to live with her. I want to hear my little-girl voice ask why and plead with them to stay together. I still want to hear my father say sorry for not waving to me, that he was hurt and vexed and too angry with my mother to wave goodbye to my sister and I. I still want to say goodbye to my friends and the dogs, and especially to my favourite guava tree, and be asked if I want to take the swing with me. Then I want someone, the truck driver or my mother, to narrate the drive away from what was home, to point out the landmarks, describe the scene as the truck speeds on, to remind me whether the sky was pale blue, whether the day was hot or was there a slight breeze, and remind me what I was wearing. I want to unfreeze the memory and expand it so my fear can melt, and I can let out my breath and know that although I did lose some things, I also gained another life.

Little four-and-a-half-year-old girl, let go now, surrender that space, move into the zephyr of your own knowing, move into the opportunity to reach new branches and claim another tree, this time a mango tree, as your refuge and talisman. Come on little four-and-a-half-year-old girl, there will always be trees wherever you go.

2. Mango Tree

The bus stops near a great big cotton tree, just off the main road. The sun has just set, and dusk steps forward. My mother climbs down the steps of the bus. A man lifts my sister and I down. The ground seems far below. Then two men help my mother with our two suitcases and a very large hamper basket. Cars zoom by so fast the gusts of air they disturb almost topple me over. A man who disembarks from the bus with us carries the two suitcases across the street, while my mother is in the middle, between my sister and I, clutching our hands, guiding us safely to the other side. She stands us way over on the soft-shoulder and tells us to stay there, while she recrosses the street to get the hamper that is taller than

I am. The man runs across the street and helps her. Back by us, the man says:

"Someone gwane meet you, m'am? You have quite a load. No way you one can manage wid de two likkle one and dem luggage."

"Yes, someone is coming to meet us, but thanks for your help," my mother replies, smiling at the man. I see her white teeth. The man walks off, in the same direction as the bus, but on the opposite side of the road. Soon he disappears into the darkness. There are no street lights. My stomach is in cramps. Cane-fields frame both sides of the road. In the distance I can hear a river gurgling. Mosquitoes nip at my legs. Few cars zoom by. We are in nowhere land. I can hardly see the road in front of us. I squeeze my legs together, wondering if Mummy would be mad if pee runs down and stains my legs, wetting my nice white lace socks and patent black shoes, not to mention my yellow panties, almost the same colour as my nylon dress with lace around the collar. I squeeze Mummy's hand, and she knows. She takes me a little ways from our things, and I squat and pee by the side of the road, urine splattering my socks and shoes. We go back to where my sister stands quietly. I hug her around the waist. We wait. We wait. We wait. Every time we hear a sound, we step forward hoping it's a car, someone to get us, but no one appears. My mother paces.

After what seems like an eternity I ask, "Mummy, is where this?"

"Caymans Estate. It's where we going to be living now. I have to be at work tomorrow morning."

My breath catches. It is Sunday night. I know this because we went to church that morning, and we are still dressed in our church dresses. We had a nice dinner with Mummy's friend, my sister's godmother, with whom we had been staying since we moved out from Daddy. After church that morning the truck came and took all of our things again. Someone was to have come and gotten us in a car after three o'clock dinner. We waited and then Mummy decided we would take the bus and the rest of our things. How hard could it be? She had laughed when Aunt Ezime, her friend, had questioned the wisdom of doing this. I wonder: "If Mummy is going to work, who will take care of my sister and I?" but I am too afraid to ask.

As if reading my fear, Mummy says, "Don't worry, Bea is at our new house unpacking. I know she is wondering where we are."

My sister and I hold hands and skip around Mummy. Bea is our nursemaid from when I was a little, little baby. My sister and I had thought we were never going to see her again after we left Daddy's house. She has a honey-brown, round face and she smells like fresh-baked bread. Bea always lifts me up and cradles me to her squishy breasts that I like to press. However, our joy is short-lived, because after waiting what feels like many, many hours, Mummy decides that it's getting late so we have to make our own way there. I don't dare ask where because I cannot see the road under my feet. I wonder how Mummy is going to carry the two suitcases and the hamper. She tells my sister and I to try and pull the hamper, each holding on to the handles at the side, but it is too heavy and large for us; my sister is six and a half years old, and I am less than a month to being five.

"Leave it and come," my mother orders, gripping the two suitcases in each hand, with us following at her heels.

My sister and I hold each other's hand firmly and I jog to keep pace with Mummy, not able to see anything in front or behind us, not even the hamper, when I glance behind. I don't know how far we walk before Mummy stops, puts down the suitcases, put us to sit on them, while she walks back and gets the hamper. My teeth chatter. My sister and I sit on one of the suitcases and cling to each other tightly, trembling as we watch Mummy get swallowed up by the night. The cane-fields swish, and darkness wraps itself around us like dirt around a coffin.

"Mummy!" my sister and I squeal in unison, when Mummy appears, panting, hauling the hamper.

I don't know how many times we walked ahead, then Mummy put down the suitcases, my sister and I holding our breath until she returned. The last thing I remember about that night is Mummy carrying me in her arms because I was too tired to walk any more, and my sister hanging on to her dress. I vaguely remember reaching the house, someone taking me from my mother's arms and putting me in bed.

I wake the next morning; the sun is glaring and I hear Bea humming. When I find my way to the kitchen she scoops me up in her arms, kisses me all over and says, "Me tiny-tiny baby wake."

I circle my arms so tightly around her neck she has to loosen them. Then she takes me into her lap and even though I can feed myself, (I was often indulged and fed even by my mother, everyone so concerned about how small I am) she spoon-feeds me oatmeal porridge, my favourite, and freshly grated and boiled hot cocoa, the filmy oil swimming on the top.

"Yu Mummy gwane work already," Bea declares as she feeds me.

I know my sister is still asleep on the bed where I left her. After eating, I walk out into a great backyard, and at the far, far rear, near the fence is a large Bombay mango tree, which quickly became my place to go off and play by myself and think and listen to the canal just beyond the fence, where some of the best mangoes landed.

Years later, I discovered that the journey from the bus to our house was a mile and a half, and for most of the way my mother carried me, placing my sister and I on one of the suitcases, then circling back to pull the larger hamper. Finally, only a half a mile from the house, she abandoned the hamper, too tired to be bothered any more. The hamper was recovered, untouched, the next day, and it was discovered that the message to meet us had not been delivered to the driver.

3. Bare Tree

Immigrating to New York from Jamaica when I was sixteen years old felt like a combination of my first two childhood moves. I was numbed. I was angry. I was traumatized. I did not want to be there, not any of the five years I lived there, even though I accomplished a lot, including earning a B.A. degree, and finding my voice as a poet. My brother and I arrived in April, the night before a snowstorm. My mother had moved there six months earlier and my sister was left in Jamaica to complete her exams. Anyone familiar with the movie *Cool Runnings* will know my response to the cold weather from those characters' chagrin. I never got warm, not even in the sweltering summers. New York appeared a cold place in more ways than one. It was the first time

I ever lived in an apartment, where strangers entered through the same front door; the first time when from the safety of my bedroom, I could hear my neighbours arguing or talking, even though, often, I could not understand what they were saying as they spoke Spanish, coming from Puerto Rico or the Dominican Republic; it was the first time I had to take public transportation and make my way to school on my own; the first time that no one on the street where I lived knew my name or greeted me, "Hello Miss Palmer's daughter, or Little Miss Palmer or Likkle Bit." I felt like an alien, moving around in a hostile place where no one spoke the language I spoke. My ears quickly learned to decipher how they said the same words differently; it sounded like they were masticating food in their mouths. Moving to New York was having to put up with ignorance from some white people and even some blacks who thought Jamaicans didn't necessarily live in houses, and weren't sure where in Africa the island was to be found. It was the first time I was specifically told not to trust anyone, and not to take anything from anyone as it was probably laced with dope and I would die.

Yet in many ways, moving to New York took the bite out of the whole idea of moving. I felt certain that I would be moving more, and I realized that regardless of where I went, I would be okay; I would meet new friends, and find a tree even if it was in a public place like Central Park, and it didn't bear fruits.

4. *Always a Tree*

As an adult, I love moving into a new house, and over the last twenty years I have moved seven times, the latter four times with one, then two, then three children and all their stuff – for two of those moves with a husband. Moving is not so bad – really. Despite having over 500 books that I still drag around with me, regardless of how much I have going on, teaching full-time, taking care of my kids, performing, etc, every box is emptied and dumped, and everything put away in its place in a month or less, tops. Most people I speak with dread moving and consider it one of the most traumatic moments in their lives. I welcome the opportunity to move. I don't want to live in any house for more than ten years ever again. While I don't like packing up, I love unpacking and deciding where pictures are to be hung, furniture is to be placed. Mostly I cherish the opportunity to discard some of the old stuff that I was once so fond of holding on to – books, magazines, birthday cards, even furniture – to make room for the new things. Every time I move I get rid of more, yet my house is still full of stuff. I am hoping that by the time I die, my children will have nothing to get rid of because I will have whittled my possessions down to just the basics. I see pictures of Japanese minimalist homes and I crave such freedom. I love travelling and have gone off with very little, and in every place, regardless of the continent or the people, I have found people who welcome me and trees that greet me. I want to be able to move in less than an hour, to bundle my things and walk, to reconnect with my ancestors, the Efe of the Congo, who were so ecologically smart, they knew that permanency was a misnomer and moved constantly, finding whatever they needed wherever they went, especially the honey that they savoured.

I see a little girl standing by the half-opened door. Her body is partially hidden by the wall; her forehead is pressed against the screen. I know tiny square-shapes are imprinted on her forehead from the mesh-wire. She is silent, but her eyes are open wide, looking out and looking inward. I think she might be eight, but she might be as young as six.

For years I have carried that little girl around in my head, telling myself she is no one I know, at least no one real. I have convinced myself that she must be a character from a movie or a dream. She is not real although she looks a lot like me, and she is leaning against the frame of the door leading to the yard from the enclosed back veranda of a house in which I used to live, leaning in a way I used to lean. But I still insist, I do not know, do not know, do not know her, I will not own that little girl.

Children must be seen and not heard
Children must be seen and not heard

That lesson from my childhood is chiselled on my mind. All children in my community were instructed in this maxim, and knew that to disregard it would prompt a quick, sharp, backhand from one's mother or a dressing-down by an adult. In silence we accepted the charges – just or unjust – levelled against us; in silence we bore the punishment that was our fate – it was for our own good, after all; in silence we watched and participated in the double standards and hypocrisy; in silence.

Still, I wasn't ready to know that little girl standing by the door. She was too close. Instead, I remembered Beverley, who at ten, before she started her menses, told Vivian and I, her best friends, that she had sex (she didn't use the word sex; I can't remember exactly how she phrased it, but it amounts to the same thing) with her seventeen-year-old neighbour whenever her mother, a nurse, was on the night shift. Apparently, the sleep-in-maid sneaked in her own boyfriend and then locked the door to her room; as a result, this boy, whose house was adjacent to Beverley's, was able to creep over, undetected. He was one of five orphaned brothers who lived with their single, eldest brother of twenty-six. Vivian and I told Beverley she was lying, making up stories. It was too outrageous for us ten year olds to believe. When Beverley said, "Some white slimy stuff came out me pussy after him pushed him ting in me, then pull eh out...", we knew for sure she was lying.

"What white stuff?"

"No way no white stuff can come out of anyone!"

Vivian and I talked about Beverley behind her back, accused her of making up stories. We concluded that, like us, she must have had a crush on what's-his-name. I don't remember his name, even though we saw him daily during the school term. He never spoke to us young, giggling girls. Surely Beverley was lying.

I never told my mother about what Beverley said.

Vivian never told her mother what Beverley said.

Beverley never told her mother what what's his name did to her whenever she was on the night shift.

I don't think any of us told anyone else. We were good little girls. We were loved. We valued being thought good little girls

When I was twelve, I remember about seven or more of us girls, ranging in age from eight to sixteen, whispering about E., the East Indian man, who hid by the outhouse of the cane-workers' house, and who always took out his thing (penis, but we would never dare use that word) whenever one of us girls passed by. We exclaimed about its largeness and fumed at his impertinence in suggestively sticking out his tongue and pursing his lips at us. We all agreed to run very fast and never go to him when he called any of us. I was surprised when one of the girls said he also did this to women. She overheard her mother talking with a woman friend about how *slack* E. was. However, when the mother realized her daughter was listening, she told her to keep her ears out of grownup business and go outside and play. Until that moment, I thought E. only hid and showed his thing to us girls. I don't remember any woman in the community warning us against taking a short cut through the cane-workers' yard, or playing hide-n-seek there or watching out for E. with his big hood always held in his hand, pointed at us. The news that E. also exposed himself to grown women was very disturbing. I quietly pondered this revelation. I didn't know the language with which to ask my mother about these things, and I am certain none of the other girls did either. We were instructed and constantly reminded:

137

Obedient children were seen but not heard.
Good children must be seen but not heard.

That was as far as I was willing to travel in the area of child abuse: memories of others like Beverley, or of me as an onlooker in a group, never as a victim. I needed to remember my childhood as happy and carefree. How could I insist that it was happy if I had been the victim of an outrageous, unspeakable crime. Had I been? Had I been molested too? Such an admission was fraught with far too many ramifications concerning people I love, a community that nurtured me, the way I see/saw myself, and how I created and continue to create myself to myself as well as to the outside world. I would not remember. I could not, would not own that little girl. Better she remain an unconnected image, a memory of a character I saw in a film or read about in some book, anyone other than me.

I would probably have buried my memories forever if one female student in my creative writing class hadn't broken down and read her memory of being raped by her high-school teacher. Another student, male, related going to a party with some friends where he drank too much and submitted to being fondled by a man as old as his father. These were memories provoked by an invitation to explore a painful moment from childhood. These sharings by my students prodded my own recollection. I could not refuse my memories any longer. I had to own them. Reluctantly, I travelled back to that first time a man abused me. I was amazed at his silent assurance and my quiet submission. No words were spoken. No threats issued. No promises made. Just silence. I saw myself with my body rigid as a statue as his hand probed beneath my dress, prying my legs apart. The entire world appeared silent, except this act was all in the open.

Children must be seen and not heard.
Children must be seen and not heard.

Owning the incident prompted the following poem that came out coded. I still wasn't able to pronounce my pain plainly, but writing the poem allowed me to breathe.

voices
inside my head everyone accusing
i was not a nicelittlegirl

138

first memory
seven
richard
my next-door neighbour's uncle

at three
i tell my daughter
to tell me
if someone   anyone
touches
her private parts even if
they threaten to kill her   me

my breath longs to escape
he thrusts me on the bed lies on top of me
pushes his tongue a rubbery plug
in my gagging mouth
i taste cigarette
he said nothing
i had no words
but the curtain fluttered
and i heard my childhood friend
talking in the kitchen
with her mother
she came back
her uncle thrust her on the bed
laid on top of her
laughing in play
after he left
my eyes caught hers
but i couldn't find the fun
we resumed our play   hushed
shrill voices denouncing us

whenever my children have been
out of my sight and return
irritable   silent
i ask and search for signs

second memory
nine
my mother is at a meeting
my sister is doing homework in the bedroom
a teenager who is watching us
invites me to play
pulling me unto his lap tickle-tickle
giggle-giggle clammyhandonmyrosebud
nipple graspingfingers   snakingintomy panty
my eyes fix on the television screen
i hear my sister's breathing i listen out for my mother
i hold my breath

third incident
respected for his age   sought for his wisdom
admired as a widower raising two daughters
a friend of my mother's
he appears this Sunday afternoon
of unlocked doors   windows wide open
i politely give him a glass of water
to catch his breath   he says
i sit on his lap like he invites
i think i hear the music coming from the piano
but my mother isn't playing
I am at home alone
yet people are everywhere
voices loud cheerful
he pulls me on his bony knees
i can't smell anything
sitting awkward wanting to run outside and play
his handpullsasidemy panty
he pushesandtriestoforcehardhoodinside me
no   words
just   breathing

don't sit on any man's lap   i warn my daughters

my mother never asked me

if anyone touched me
no adult ever asked
everyone assumed
i was safe
i didn't need to know
the language of my protection
but muzzled fear stole my defence
i will tell my children
about the power of silence
the touches punctuated with
pleas   threats   warnings
the silence that makes you an accomplice
of your own violation
bold looks
that inform you
i'm touching you because
you   want   me   youwantmeto
let's pretend   nothing
is happening with your body
body b o d y body

I can now say with certainty that four different men abused me
at least five times. The first time I was probably seven years old. I
was standing by the veranda door and handed soap to the plumber
who had just fixed our plugged-up drain. My mother was at work,
and Jean, our maid, was somewhere in the house. The plumber
washes his hand at the pipe affixed to the side of the house. When
he is done, he returns the soap, but just that quickly his hand
lingers, travelling down, under my dress, pulling my panty aside.
I wondered if Jean or anyone else was observing him fondling me.
I wanted someone to shout at him to stop. I wondered why he
chose me, what had I done to make him feel it was safe to put his
dirty hand under my dress. I wanted to call out to Jean, but I had
no voice. Then he was gone. I wanted to tell my mother, but I
didn't. I remembered when I was about five years old, Jean caught
one of my playmates and I playing house outside in the backyard
under the mango tree. William just wanted to show me what he
observed his parents doing the night before. He straddled me and

rubbed his groin area up and down. We were pulled apart; he was slapped on the bottom, told he was a rude boy and sent summarily home. I was taken inside and put to bed. When my mother returned from work, William's and my game was reported to her. I remember how serious and stern she was as she talked to me, Jean looking on, saying "Nice little girls didn't do that sort of thing," and making me promise that I would not play that way with William or any boy again. I wasn't punished, but I remember trying to figure out what I had done, and why it made me a bad little girl. But I didn't inquire, and neither my mother nor Jean offered any further explanation. The lesson, however, was internalized.

When I was about nine and half, I remember my mother attending a meeting and having N. the pastor's teenage son, baby-sit my sister and I. Everyone in the community spoke well of N. whose character, they professed, was exemplary. I remember him helping my sister and me with our homework, then after a while my sister went into the bedroom to read. N. and I were left in the living room. He started to tickle me; I tickled him back and we rolled around on the floor laughing. Then he sat on the sofa, turned on the television and pulled me to sit in his lap, my legs over the arm of the sofa. Slowly N. started to touch me, his clammy hand caressing my rosebud breasts. Then he lifted up my dress, arranged it over his lap, then he pulled back my panty, his finger probing inside my pussy. I sat very still, focusing on my sister's breathing and shuffling of paper in the bedroom, my eyes glued to the television screen, yet not seeing or hearing the programme going on in front of my eyes. I sat on N.'s lap for a long, long time, with his fingers in my pussy and my eyes transfixed. What struck me then was the stillness of the house. I felt everything was on pause, like me with my breath sucked in. I made sure to be seen, but not heard.

Mr. C. was a widower, a respected senior admired for raising his two daughters after his wife died. He was in his fifties when he fathered his daughters and they were teenagers the day he came over to our house. He was a friend of my mother and often visited, stopping to have a cool drink, especially at Christmas when, he remarked, she made the best sorrel drink. It was not unusual for someone to stop at our house and ask for a drink of water on a hot day. One would not refuse anyone water, even a stranger, and certainly not a family friend. Mr. C. appeared this Sunday afternoon while a cricket match was being played at the club, just 300 yards from my house. I was sitting on the front steps daydreaming. Mr. C. greeted me then asked for a tall glass of water as the day was so hot and he had been out walking. I invited him to sit in the living room while I went into the kitchen to fetch him the water. He drank slowly, sitting in the leather armchair by the open window that looked out into the front yard. I could feel his eyes on me. He rested the half-empty glass on the bookcase to his right and asked me where everyone was. I told him they were at the cricket match. He patted his lap and told me to come and sit with him as he wanted to hear about school. He knew I was a bright and good little girl. I complied, sitting on his lap and answering all his questions. Then I felt him squirming and his hand fumbling in his lap. Suddenly, something hard was being rubbed and pushed up against my bottom.

I see myself sitting like a good little girl – almost ten years old, my hands folded in my lap, my lips pulled tight as he rubbed and tried to force his penis through the leg of my panty. We heard voices. Mr. C. quickly reached for the water, emptied the glass in one gulp, then patted and thanked me for being such a good girl, and helping to quench an old man's thirst. *Children must be seen and not heard, children must be seen and not heard*

The last incident occurred when I was around twelve. Karen and her family had moved, but R. still lived in the neighbourhood. He had in fact impregnated one of our maids, but took no financial responsibility for their child. Rumour had it that he had several other children throughout the community. This particular mid-week evening, while my mother had gone to get my sister from her piano lesson, and I sat on the back veranda doing my homework, R. came into the house (the door as usual was unlocked) asked me where everyone was, then when he was certain I was alone, he bent on his knees, crawled under the table where I sat, pried my legs open and proceeded to finger me. Pretending as if nothing out of the ordinary was taking place, I sat trying to do my homework, while R. dug away inside of me. I felt as if the entire community was watching him there on his knees, under the table, his fingers scraping the walls of my vagina. I could hear the community's unanimous rebuke that I was a bad girl.

I can't say exactly how many minutes R. knelt under the table finger-fucking me or even when he left, but I remember for the first time feeling a fear I had not felt before. I knew then that the only way I could protect myself from him and others was through concealment.

It got so that whenever I was home alone, and I heard footsteps I would hide in some corner hoping it wasn't R. or Mr. C. or some other man who felt secure enough to pull my panty aside and dig his finger into me. I learned from talking to the other girls my age, and from overhearing some of the older girls talking, that Mr. C. also pinched their breasts, rubbed his penis on them, and finger-fucked them too, and just like me they never told their parents. None of us told our mothers.

Initially I had believed it was because my mother was a single parent, because our home was one of the few households without a father that men preyed on my sister and me. However, I learned of other girls whose fathers lived at home, who were also prey to Mr. C., R., E. and nameless other men. It seemed that almost all girls were prey, if not to direct fondling, then tongues stuck out suggestively, or whistling or crude remarks said in earshot to get our attention.

I can't help but wonder now at the perversity of a society in which child abuse was and is so rampant. What is it about the way this culture views sexuality that prompts such action in so many men, many of whom are considered "decent", law-abiding citizens? Equally alarming are the codes of the society that silence children, especially girl-children, to surrender to abuse and internalize their violation as their personal shame, as though something in their behaviour solicited or prompted such actions. Paedophilia is rampant. What is it about this culture that causes so many adults to sexually prey on children? My mother and the other women of my community never knew how to protect me or any of the other girls from being sexually preyed on, even though they surrounded us with love. But their silence made us victims. They, as women, were themselves victims, constantly deflecting attack.

For too long I carried my burden, locked in silence. I cherished being thought of as a good girl so I couldn't tell anyone about my fear and pain. I believed I was responsible for those men's actions towards me. But I know now that I did not invite that plumber, or R., or N., or Mr. C. They came like bold, daring thieves, robbing my innocence and they walked away, heads high, proud of their crime. Now I know that little girl, who has been, for thirty-odd years, my shadow stalking my tracks. She is no longer mute or silent.

I see that little girl. I see her.

Standing by the half-opened door.

Being thrown on her girlfriend's bed.

Sitting on a young man's lap, the television going.

Sitting on an old man's lap, the curtain at the open window sailing like a runaway kite.

I embrace that little girl. She is me. I hear her. I hear me. My cry sounds. My pain begins to dissipate. I will never again pretend that I don't know that hurt little girl inside me. So I name yet forgive all the men who touched my body and made me feel shame. I name the plumber, R., N., Mr. C.. I denounce and forgive them. I reproach all the men and women who touch children inappropriately and abuse them, causing children to feel shame, silencing them and leaving them always vulnerable. I name and pray for the redemption of all those who abuse, and all those who would abuse, so children will never have to feel shame again, will never be silenced any more, will never any more have to wail out in the middle of the night when an affectionate touch triggers painful memory.

children must be seen and heard, seen and heard
children must speak out
and their voices heard
they must shout without fear
we must hear them
and act in their defence
we must no longer silence
children to abuse
children must be seen and heard, seen and heard
children must never be silenced…

SHE SCRAPE SHE KNEE:
THE THEME OF MY WORK
(1989)

As a girl I often scraped my knee, not because I had poor balance or tripped over my feet but because I dared to be more, or other, than what good girls were supposed to be. I was never a good girl, and I passionately disliked those girls who were, and loathed their dull expressions. Nice girls never scraped their knees.

As a woman I am often scraping my knee, sometimes without even falling. Perhaps it is because I dare to demand that the way be cleared for me or that I insist on leading the line at times. My choice. Always. Now as I reflect, I see that there is much in common between the little girl who frequently scraped her knee, and has scars to prove it, and this woman, me, who must often walk stiff-legged in defiance of the scrapes that are inflicted, often by the insensitive, the blind, the upholders of norms, traditions, and antiquated values that I had no part in setting and by which I will not abide. I scrape my knee.

I have found that among my female friends, knee-scrapers tip the scale. We are so abundant with our songs, our plays, our poems, our paintings, our research, our cameras, and our children that all of us continuously scrape our knees and will not stop, even though we are not masochistic. But doing what we do, in the society in which we live, demands payment for our disregard of the law – Women, know thy place and thy place is often in the kitchen or horizontally disposed. Let me hasten to add that I find both positions appealing at times, but choice is the operative mode in this regard. So we scrape our knees.

To lack scars on one's knees means one has lived safely, followed the rules, not questioned authority, accepted the pre-scribed rules. Since an energy within does not allow me to believe in blind destiny, I find that I constantly scrape my knees but make marvellous discoveries and have great fun in the process. More important, each time I scrape my knee I learn about my potentials as well as my limitations, and I experience the Mother-God within me. So I celebrate my scraped knees. Now I worry if I go for extended periods unscathed. Fortunately, the nosy child is still around in the form of an inquisitive, eavesdropping woman so, alas, pussy scars always grace my knees.

As a writer I don't set out to scrape anyone's knees. I do not want to see anyone have to buckle under and stumble; I do not want to see anyone have to rub cocoa butter on his or her knees to fade away the dark crust; I do not want to see anyone have to grit teeth, shrug off the resistance, and walk on stiff legs. But alas, even in my writing I find that both my readers and I scrape knees. Born in Jamaica, a very class- and colour-conscious society, I watched many women scrape their knees, often without knowing why they were felled, and often not being allowed a moment to acknowledge the pain or massage the swelling. These were the women who were the most beautiful to me, their beauty more a part of their defiance and independence than such physical whims as nose, mouth and eye size, length of hair, or colour of skin. So unknowingly I vowed to be a knee-scraper and this journey was begun.

To be a writer is to be arrogant, to assume that your "truth" is more valuable, more insightful than that of non-writers; to write is to commit sin to print, pain to inspection, joy to the communal table. But this is one side; the other side of being a writer is to be humble, to have the desire to share a joy, a pain, a vision not yet realized, sometimes not even formulated. A writer is a person with vision, a seer, a mouthpiece for the voiceless, the mute, as well as an observer of the talker, the braggart, the fool. Writers all scrape their knees.

Although definitions more often limit than elucidate who or what is being addressed, I will join the rank of definers and say I am a Caribbean feminist writer who attempts to highlight the small, to amplify quiet rooms, to thrust the skeleton from the closet, to make noise, to portray more than I see, and to render the ordinary in all its extraordinary simplicity. What this means is that I am specifically concerned with women, men, and children and their ability to cohabit and to create a world that is clean, safe, and open to differences; I am interested in planting the idea that equality is an appreciation of all of our talents, an act of love and faith in each other's ability to receive and give love; that a commitment to equality means to agree, understand, and fight for everyone else's opportunity to be heard. This is particularly crucial in the Caribbean context, where neocolonialism wears a perfumed head. We all scrape our knees.

My work is shaped by my childhood experience, and though I have lived in North America for many years, my roots remain buried in the red bauxite soil of Jamaica. I still drink cassava soup and eat breadfruit. In my work I attempt to illuminate the myths, to reveal a picture of Caribbean life that is too real for commercials, to reclaim our land and remove us from being simply the property of someone else's dream vacation. I am concerned about neocolonialism and expansionism as exemplified by the invasion of Grenada in 1983; I am concerned about the shortages of schools for our children; I am concerned that my great-grand-aunt Zilla, living in rural St. James, still does not have running water and must walk two miles to the nearest bus. I am deeply concerned that poor women must bring their own linen to the public hospital and lie two to a single bed after giving birth; I am concerned that within the last five years the increase in the numbers of brutal rapes of women and girls, some as young as ten, has skyrocketed and there has been very little outcry from the society; I am deeply concerned that young men are unemployed, left to prowl the streets and hang out at sound systems to try to catch a glimpse of their dreams; I am very concerned that our little piece of the rock, independent as we claim to be, is only so on paper and that we still look to metropolitan countries to set standards of beauty, value, and cultural validation. We crawl, we creep, we walk, we stumble, we scrape our knees.

My writing is an attempt to grapple with what it means to be a woman, black, Caribbean, conscious. These are not different realities; they are integrated. I cannot emphasize the wholeness enough. Too often nothing gets accomplished because we separate into camps and compartmentalize our experiences based on an internalization of our Euro-American education. I am symphonic, and whatever I process is integrated in myself as a woman, a person of African descent, a Caribbean. Like the tree of which I am a branch, I am perennial. I am certain of my continuation even though the form might alter to adapt to a new climate. I/we will be around because we are knee-scrapers, survivors of the seas and wind, reapers of cane and banana, makers of history.

I am a bird-of-paradise, partly through heritage but mostly by example, and I must admit that my examples were almost always women who never showed any diffidence in the face of adversity. I associate the carnival colours of my girlhood with these women, who were as captivating as the yellow poui blossoms, breathtaking as the flame-red flamboyant, and bittersweet as sugar-cane. My short story collection, *Bake-Face and Other Guava Stories*, is a tribute to those women who never have access to microphones, who carry their madness sewed into their skirt hems and tied in the handkerchiefs buried in their bosoms. Giving voice to this madness that besieges us, giving voice to the celebration of our lives, giving voice to our quiet fears and invisible tears, giving voice to our struggles, our victories, our determination, I scrape my knee, she scrapes her knee, we all scrape our knees.

Perhaps I was only seven years old when I first heard Louise Bennett, the Jamaican Queen Mother of verse and humour, recite her poetry. Her voice was resonant and sure, rendering our speech musical, classic, poetic, the rhythm that my prep school was teaching me was the voice of the uneducated masses, and therefore inappropriate. I faltered in my boastful stance that my "proper" speech was enviable, to be admired. Here was Louise Bennett, clearly more proper, more eloquent. I remember my surprise that such a bold knee-scraper was allowed to flaunt her sassiness, her tenacity, her affirmation of herself and us. But later I was to learn that knee-scrapers are never allowed anything, that we seize the moment, the day. Louise Bennett stole the time, and this created a space for me. And perhaps it was then that I decided to use our rhythms in my poetry, my stories, in the recording of our lives. It gives colour and flavour and validates our cultural ethos. Bennett allowed me to be brave and risk the surprised satisfaction of being myself.

To say that I am chronicling our lives would seem to limit my role to that of a historian. Although I believe that all conscientious writers are historians, the good writer is more: a sociologist, psychologist, architect, musician, cane-cutter, pallbearer, and recorder. My work emerges from the core of my life – my family – from which I weave the memories that we think we no longer know with the memories that we forgot we had with the memories that are alive! As such my writing is encompassing and circuitous, no separation between the past, the future, and this moment.

I am the work, and the work is woman, womanish, leggo; I am female child of Catherine, sister of Leonie (aka Dawn, her family pet name), aunt of Paul Patrick, mother of Shola Yetunde. I am woman, but more, more to my sisters, whose hands, rough from scrubbing clothes and pounding yam, cry out. I am wo/man, womanish. My mother used to declare, threatening/applauding, "Two 'oman can't live in de same house." I, woman, knew I had to comfort the mother who walked away from the drunkard husband and received a slap for daring to be independent and be her own boss when most other women sucked in their lips and mumbled under their breaths; a mother who lived feminism before the word was current coinage and came to be a label, a badge of honour, disrepute, and struggle. I am female, black, mother, lover, writer, student going against the tides, daring anyone to step in my path, swimming in Yemoja's waves, calling on Oshun, remembering Ida B. Wells, fighting with Mary Nyarijiru, Mau Mau warrior, echoing Sojourner Truth's words, "Ain't I a woman?" Questions they asked for me. Questions! They sacrificed for me. Nanny, the Maroon warrior, caught bullets in her teeth and made magic from soil. Miss Scott put three husbands in the grave and was so stern that the most vicious bulldog hid his tail in her presence and crawled to safety in a corner. Who paints their stories? Who writes songs in memory of their lives? Who acknowledges their contributions? Their bravery ensures that fewer knees get scraped.

I am the work, and the work is womanish. The stories are of these many-varied women, acknowledging that there is not just one kind of woman; what they have in common is their strength, their determination to be their own bosses, to push their girl-women ahead with education, economic independence, and birth control. My work is for the market women whose pride is always borne on their heads; for the prostitutes leaning on the walls of Kingston dying for day to break so they can hurry home to make porridge for their children and send them off to school with the money they collected by slaving; for the women who are intimately connected to men and nurture them and are loved and abused by them; for the girl-women forced by lack of class privilege to grow up too fast; for the women who have always danced with the sun and felt the wind caress their hair; for the girls trying to defend themselves against images in advertising that would constrain and categorize them, while claiming to be for their liberation. My work celebrates women's need to be loved, to have sex, to be wild and crazy if the occasion calls for it. My poems are womanish, female, spirited, sponging Winnie Mandela's feet, rubbing the shoulders of the basket women in Kenya, raising the backs of Indian women; my writing is an introduction into a world of womanism. Scrape, scrape, we are scraping knees.

THE ECHO OF WORDS
(2006)

Words are like the saliva on my tongue. Without moisture I cannot talk, without writing I cannot live, at least not in any meaningful way. I write out of love, a need deeper than the bluest ocean, a need connected to my marrow, surging through my blood, pumping life from my heart, streaming down the Rio Cobre, misting the Blue Mountains, snaking its way through Fern Gully, and flowing down Dunns River Falls. I am my land, the people whose bodies sheltered and nourished me to life. I am their stories; their tales ring in my ears, calling to me at every turn saying, "Is my time now, you know; is fi we time. What you waiting on? Why you not telling them about we? Why you playing the fool? Sit down, child, sit down and write me now; write we."

They come to me anytime, at the oddest times, at all times, popping into my head, stealing and even usurping the very moment to which I am supposed to be present. Suddenly, I am into their life, the distant past, where they had no one to listen to them, no one to write their life, but they are fiercely determined – will not die a silent death. In me they find the willing listener they have been seeking. I don't turn from them or close my ears; I don't dismiss them as insignificant. I listen, I inquire, I probe, and I nod my head to indicate that I understand. Most importantly, I show myself to be curious, even eager to hear, to know, to grasp the full meaning of who and what they are. Of greater significance, I believe them. I know that what they say, what they have experienced is a history that needs recording, that they have given me the truth I have been seeking and that others need to hear their tale so that they might come to know themselves more fully. I see the bravery of their small lives; I understand the significance of the roles they played in life and thus realize that it is this connection that possessed them to attach themselves to me because in me they have found not just a willing listener, but also an able defender, a champion of the meaning of the space they have opened for others.

Often it is nature that awakens the writing spirit in me – some aspect of nature takes me outside of myself to see and be witness to a larger truth, to welcome characters, people I have never met into my life. Sometimes my eyes are arrested by a butterfly flitting in my garden or a dog sitting under a tree, tongue hanging; sometimes it is a lizard, belly-bound, crawling on the barbed-wire fence, orange-flame tongue extended like lightning to catch a fly; other times it is just the rays of the sun toasting my arms or it is the way the breeze rustles the trees, or the movements of the clouds shifting shape into something I am not yet able to identify, or the chirping of birds, and sometimes, it is just sitting still, being open to life – hearing a voice, or seeing things, and knowing something that I didn't know, until I know it at the oddest moments. Oftentimes it is just allowing life to come to me, to be me, to be willing to be a vehicle, another eye, a gong from the past, a rumble announcing the future.

The influences are numerous and everywhere, but on a conscious level my writing is motivated and influenced by history, by the role black people presently occupy on the continent and throughout the Caribbean and the Americas, by having an instinctive sense that I am connected viscerally and genetically to something much larger than can be seen with the naked eye or comprehended by the limits of our minds, something larger, grander, yet as ordinary as our breath. My writing is attracted and attached to history – herstory – those details and perspectives that have not yet been written, the connections that have not yet been drawn, the gaps that have not yet been filled.

Certain images and people keep appearing to me and they refuse to go away. I don't remember inviting them, but they show up at my door, knock loudly and will not be turned back. I sometimes pretend that I am not home, hide out inside my own head. It is like glimpsing someone in the street you want to avoid, so you turn inside a store, or appear to be deeply absorbed by the window display, biding time, until you hope the person you were avoiding has passed. But just as you turn around, letting out your breath, you find the person directly in front of you so you fake a smile, allow yourself to be engaged by small talk, or you mumble apologies about how much in a hurry you are, and hope they will allow you to escape. However, everywhere you turn they are there. The people I write about quickly become my friends, some of whom I like and care about deeply, and some I am just annoyed by, impatient with, want them to just go and sit down and figure something out before coming back to me. Some of the characters do take my advice and go off and then reappear again and I am often surprised by what they have learned, because sometimes it is the very thing I don't want to learn or hear – notions of forgiveness, endurance, long-suffering, compassion. But no matter how I try to ignore them, no matter how long I lock myself inside and pretend not to hear their knocking, they are unmoving. When I open the door the following morning or even a year later, they are still there sitting quietly, serenely on my patio, greeting me as if I hadn't been ignoring them, telling me how lovely I look, and how glad they are to see me, pretending, as I had been pretending, that I have not been barricading myself indoors to avoid them. These characters are as sweet as pone and polite as an old lady on her way to church, so that I am contrite, feel badly, apologize and listen in earnest, to all they have to say, and scold myself for having been so rude in the first place.

MY BODY AS TRANSCRIPT
(2006)

My body is a reservoir of memories, ancestral and national, that can be triggered by a touch, a voice, a fleeting occurrence in nature, or an image that the mind conjures. Yet I cannot say where on my body, certainly not only in my brain, these stories and poems are stored, or how I go about accessing them. There is no formula for awakening them. Perhaps there is mysticism in saying it just happens, that I write the yarns stored in my body. It is like finding a loose piece of thread that I try to break off, but as I pull, it unwinds.

Once, while cradling one of my sick children in my arms, I unwound an entire spool. I thought I had dozed. There I was nodding on the sofa, blanket snug around us while my mind jogged to capture the story oozing out like mucous from my child's nostrils. *Crouching in the bushes was a man, blood trickling from the left side of his head, his hand clasped tightly over a stone. His eyes contained both terror and defiance. This was not the first time he had had to run. This was not the first time he had killed, but this was the first time he had killed out of love, to protect someone other than himself, and he had scared himself. He didn't know where to go.* He wanted me to help him figure it out. Who was he and why should I write his story? He was so alone and terrified, yet here he was inviting me into his life, beckoning me to come quickly, quietly, talking about how he had been waiting a long time for me and that he only had a short time left. I had grown to understand the poems that came in the middle of lovemaking, that pulled me out of my lover's arms, even when all I wanted to do was stay locked in tight embrace. But this was altogether new. I am usually obedient – in a defiant kind of way – to these demands; if I am not, I cannot settle and enjoy what I crave – my man's arms wrapped around me, his body pressed into my back. Now, even in the midst of nursing my ill child, here was a character who could disregard my maternal desires and demand that his life be rendered real.

He took my hand firmly in his, our fingers clasped and the story was born. It was visceral and instant.

I also somehow knew this woman, even though she lived four

hundred odd years ago. *She was powerful and wealthy, admired by her community. Whenever she entered the market, voices hushed because she walked like the very ground belonged to her and her dress always billowed like butterfly wings and the colours were brilliant. The first time she saw him was at her stall, in the midst of giving directions to her two husbands in preparation for negotiating a major deal. She looked out, and for a moment, time stopped when her eyes locked with his. The air was instantly stifling and the voices ceased. There was something searing about the way his eyes stripped away, not her clothes, but what covered her thoughts and deep desires. She knew in that moment that he loved her and she would love him like she would no other man. She was only twenty-five years old when she took him as her third husband.* But she could not have seen what I, the writer, knew. *He loved her so deeply that it would cost him his life, and leave a gaping hole in her heart that she would never be able to fill, even though she would go on to take two further husbands and have four more children.* All of that just from this man taking my hand in an intimate, familiar manner.

Another time, when the day was particularly warm, I went to lie out in the sun and the rays were like feathers tracing lightly over my arms; I felt as if I was being touched from my shoulders to my elbows, and like a film's slow resolution from a dissolve, the story came to imprint its details in my mind. It is like a reel inside my head, and I am walking, actually reliving the details, being there and yet not there, an inside observer. Right away, I am making up dialogue to give him speech, and although I am certain I have not met him in this life, he lives, gigantic and three-dimensional in my head – so much so that he distracts me from the immediacy of the life I am supposed to be living with lover and children and friends and colleagues. *He walks in, dressed from head to foot, as they say, sweating in the woollen suit he wears in the afternoon heat. Standing at the pulpit, handsome and refined in appearance, he looks out ready to give the eulogy, not a song of praise but rather a strident condemnation. It is so unexpected that the family members and other mourners will be too stunned to stop him before he is done. He feels vindicated, at long last. Thirty-three years he had waited for this moment. Thirty-three years, denying himself love, denying himself his very home, because a man he had regarded as his best friend, a man for whom he would have laid down him life, went*

156

and did the unspeakable. He had used his very words, exploited his confidence and stole the only woman he had ever loved right from under him, just so, then turned around and laughed in his face, spewing a children's story about Anansi see and Anansi take, and tough luck for the man who waits. Well, now the brute, Jascet Pillars, was dead, after six months of suffering, and he, Nathaniel Joshua Thomlyn, was alive and healthy and intending to go and propose to the only woman he ever loved, the widowed Mrs. Pillars, who had suffered much from the brute of a man who tricked her into marrying him. Nathaniel chuckled as he descended the pulpit and saw the mourners, jaws slack, mouths opened, eyes wide with disbelief. He didn't care as he turned to sit beside Charmaine Pillars, but he had to suppress the laughter that bubbled in his throat, threatening to spill over as he remembered his mother's words: "Time longer than rope, me boy, time longer than rope, so don't fret youself." Nathaniel Joshua Thomlyn takes his seat beside the widow and places her hand in his, and she does not withdraw it, even though the pastor, perspiration running off his face like rain, frowns down on them, consternation crowing his face. As the writer, I have no idea yet how the pastor is going to make a comeback after Nathaniel's damning eulogy, but I am certain, given his male ego and the role in the community that he wants to secure, that he will manage to placate the family and return a modicum of decorum and sadness to meet the occasion. All this, just because the rays were feathers opening my pores, making sweat and history one on my skin.

I mine my body for stories. As a writer I must often sit at my desk and, like a miner panning for gold, go in search of the stories. I know they are there. I touch my body, I speak to it, invite it to be present. I cast the pan – sitting, arms crossed at my chest, hands stroking shoulders, chafing the ideas, massaging them alive – pulling out the pan and sieving through to find the gold – and the story glows in my head. *They are in her garden, at the far end away from the house, and although no one is in sight and the dogs are barking, she pulls her friend to stand closer to her and she whispers, "Ah know he have other woman. Is not the first, but such is a wife's lot. You have to turn deaf ears and go on. You just can't take on these men and their doggish ways. You know how it is, dog never care where he stand up and raise his hind leg to* pee. But, Millicent, a telling you, this one different, and it causing gas to gather on me chest like mildew on stale bread. Is not say I love this man, that much you know, even though we been married almost twenty-seven years now. We comfortable, and you know that I haven't worked because ah got pregnant right before we get married, and him say him didn't want him wife to work. Then every time I turn round, the man on top of me and is just so me pregnant again, seven children in thirteen years. All me time take up with keeping his house just so and taking care of his children. Is only now me have some time to do my garden like me enjoy and sit down without someone needing something. Ah like me life like how it is now. But what if this blasted old man who want to feel young decided fi leave me and marry this young woman. Me no have nothing against her. She can let him jump on top of her all she want, but me not gwane divorce him. Me not leaving this house or me garden. Me just not gwane lose what me work all these years fi secure. So Milly, what you think me must do. Me know where this woman live. You think me should go and talk to her?"

Millicent looks at her friend and wants to cry. She doesn't know what to tell her. She had known for months that Bushrod, Mavis's husband, was having an affair. She had overheard him confiding to her husband, and she knew he was planning to get a divorce and marry this young woman who was pregnant. She had known Mavis all her life, since they were three years old. Their husbands were good friends. When Mavis's children were in high school, Millicent had tried to tell her to find a job and gain some skills so she could have some money of her own, but Mavis always allowed Bushrod to talk her out of it. Now here she was, fifty years old, with no money of her own. Of course her children would take her in, but it wouldn't be the same. Millicent knew that Bushrod was not going to give up the house, and that more than likely Mavis would have to move. Millicent's sadness caused her mouth to feel as if all of her saliva had evaporated. Sometimes knowing is a burden, Millicent thought. Should she be the one to break the news to her friend? There are some stories that come from my body that I don't want to explore, the telling is too hard. Mavis's story, while sad, is not unique. But she wants space to share. I don't want to deny her the need to vent, but I am also trying to see around the bend, to see if there is a way she might triumph over this domestic lot. I continue to massage my shoulders. Like the miner, I cast the pan again, but this time after I sieve to the bottom there is no gold. I will get back to Mavis, or maybe I won't.

My body does not discriminate about where the stories are stored on it, nor about the type of story or the particulars of the character. My body is its own landscape, and each terrain houses its own memory. Sometimes the stories are rubbed out from my thighs, sometimes they are caressed to life from behind my knees, sometimes someone like a Prince Charming kisses them awake from behind my neck, or flushes them out with a probing tongue from my navel. No telling where they are hiding or when they will spring into life, demanding my attention. All I know is that my body knows; it has tributaries to the past, it has outlets to the future, it has tunnels to other lives that I can only conjure after I have found myself in those places that I didn't know existed until I got there. Then the ideas become real, and it's like: I know this place. *The saffron sautéing in the pan wafts throughout the house, with its windows partially open.* My right thumb scratches the itch in my left palm. *She is watching him, her boss, sitting by the window in his living room, observing everyone who goes by, and making copious notes in his journal. She has worked for him for six years now, and in that time she has never once seen anyone cross over to enter his house, unless she is alone. She doesn't know that he knows that she spies on him, and that he is in fact amused and gratified by her interest. Once, while he was taking a shower, she pulled out his journal from the drawer and looked in it. She could not decipher the language in which he wrote, although they spoke the same language. Yet every day, for the greater part of the afternoon, he sat by the window, noticing someone, then jotting down a few lines, often glancing from his writing to the person passing by the open window. She has seen him do this for almost as many years as she has been working for him. She doesn't know why he wants her to come every day, when clearly he doesn't need her, except to cook the two meals he has daily. He is neat and single so there is not much for her to do, except watch him watch others.* That is all the itch in my palm yields; for now that is the whole story. But my body is not done. I rub my eyes, stretch my arms above my head, rotate my shoulders and I am on to another transcript.

I know that teal dress and the shop where it was bought. I have the words that she needs to speak, and until I give them to her, she must stand there and wait, anxious but dumb, pregnant but silent. I have known her and will come to know her even more than she knows herself. I will determine her fate and how others know her and if they care about her and her small pain that is to her like a hot-air balloon. My fingertips touch the keys and sketch her life; each touch unravels more details, provides another angle of her obdurate determination in the face of her parents' obsessive love and her desire to slice off a thin fragment of her life and keep it tucked in her bra away from their scrutiny.

He touched me, lightly, a normal exchange of intention to be more than friends, and sent me wobbling. Didn't I want to be with him? Weren't we supposed to be having dinner? Did he do something wrong? Yes. No. You touched me where the memories are stored. You touched me where she lived and now she is demanding that I provide her with the outlet she has been seeking. Yes, I want to have dinner with you, and yes, I want to get to know you, but no I cannot stay, the story calls and it will not wait, but I hope you will. I want you to touch me somewhere else, another time and bring to life another character. Who knows the magic of your touch?

"Are these narratives true?" "Can a touch be false?" "Did you make them up or did they happen to you?" They happened. Senseless to inquire. Someone else, I believe, concurs with me that every lie I write is the truth. While it might not have happened (that I know of) before the idea/image popped in my head, the moment I begin writing, my body confirms the truth, takes me to the very roots of the characters' origins that are planted deep in the blood that pumps my heart. Perhaps my body lies to me. Maybe it is possessed. But I know that my body knows things, so I will not Judas my body. I will not reject it in favour of normalcy. I know that it knows. I know that it is a register upon which meticulous accounts are written and, sometimes, I am privileged to decode and access these narratives. I sometimes wonder how my body stores these new records and who will gain entry to them? I ask myself whose body have I inherited and why? Why these stories?

The tales are not only solicited by the touch of love or lust, but also from a bruise, a stumped toe, the embrace of a girlfriend, a hug from one of my children, a brush up against a stranger in a busy mall or on a packed train, the furtive glance from someone, my constant eavesdropping, my own hand against my body.

Those of the imprints on my body that I have come to know are the result of my conscious deliberations as a writer who insists on knowing, and calling the knowing of my body to task.

So when this character, whom I have literally been courting for over six years (although I have not yet committed a word of her story, not even a sketch, synopsis or profile, to paper), ends up on the beach, sitting beside and talking with one of the men who raped her and together they remember how they came, in another lifetime, on the same boat from the coast of Africa, I am outraged, undone, feel betrayed by my body's memory and resolution. I want this wanton rapist to pay. It feels as if he has gotten off too easily. This, after all, is not his story, this is her story and I want her to be a heroine for women, to usurp power for herself, but my body wants to tell it differently. My body, it seems, has its own agenda; it leaks out the details of this rapist's life that I don't really want to know because I don't want his act of terror to be excused in any way.

There are lacerations that my body doesn't want to remember, pain so sharp – the jagged edge of a bottle scraping the tongue to silence it, permanently. It is the blind running and the longing that is a blood vessel popping inside the brain. My body has pulled the blinds over some of its stories, refuses to visit that part of its storage unit, and denies me entry, although I might be allowed to peep through the dust-covered window. I have unearthed stories that are still too painful to write – I cannot yet find any joy, any light in or out of them.

My body knows the stories of an aching longing, longing for recognition, longing for loving, longing for something to happen so strong that the mind turns to sawdust. While massaging my tight calves, the girl appeared. *She is long-legged, soon to be thirteen, born on the very porch of the lone shop, in a dusty, rural town, where she now squats scanning the horizon, hopeful. Day-in-day-out, she stoops there, occasionally being roused by a customer needing milk or eggs, or a little sugar, more often only molasses. Her mama no longer nags her to go to school. Her legs are ashy and her hair needs combing, but despite the dishevelled appearance, her eyes are clean as a new moon and her face has a quiet beauty that forces a closer scrutiny.* The day I meet her, she is as always – I can tell immediately – wanting but not willing. *Squatting, one hand shielding the sun from her eyes, she peers into the distance, hoping, longing, praying this will be the day when someone, anyone new and alive comes.* I am hopeful for her; I want someone to enter her life and smile at her as much as she wants, but like her I see no one on the horizon, so I leave her there and turn my attention elsewhere, not because I am unmoved by her, but because she has not yet forced the story to unfold. My calves are no longer tight.

The phone rings and I hunch my shoulder to cradle the receiver and as he speaks something in his voice distracts me. When I hang up the phone, the boy springs from my head, stumbling over his own feet. *His granddaddy bought him a saxophone from the pawnshop, and he was so happy, although he was fifteen he threw his arms around his granddaddy and hugged him, forgetting that he was too big for that, and his granddaddy must have forgotten too, because his granddaddy kissed him on the forehead like he used to do when he was in first grade and his granddaddy took him to school. For a moment, they were both awkward, then the boy stood back, smiled up at his granddaddy who was still a good four inches taller than him, standing 6'2", and said, "Thank you, Granddaddy. You're the best. You're gonna see. I am gonna be blowing this here horn real good, real soon." Then the boy, embracing the horn to his chest, turned and ran, taking the stairs two steps at a time. Once in his room, he slammed the door, slumped on his bed, and attempted to rub away the tears attempting to creep from his eyes. He hoped one day he would make his granddaddy proud of him. He imagined his granddaddy coming to one of his concerts and hearing him blow. He had not believed that he would get the horn and it wasn't even his birthday or Christmas. The tears came anyway, and he allowed them, the horn pressed against his chest.*

I already know a lot about this boy, even though I've only just met him. I know he lives in an urban city in the USA. I know he has an African name. I know his granddaddy is from the Caribbean and played the horn as a boy, but his grandson doesn't know this. I know the boy is going to be taken places, literally every time his mouth touches the horn. The boy wants his story told. He is impatient, has a sense of urgency, unlike the girl on the porch above, for whom time is a flat expanse with no ending in sight. As the writer, it is not I who prioritize which story gets written, but rather the characters and their sense of urgency. While my body has the story, it lacks insight into some of the physical gestures and movements of this young musician, as well as knowledge about the nuances of the instrument. I must ascertain the name of great saxophone players, and I will have to listen to some of their music in order to complete the story. I will have to find and speak to someone who teaches and plays this instrument to get a better feel for the boy and his development as a naturally gifted musician, but who nonetheless initially struggles with getting the sound right. I am amazed that my body knows this boy and what he is thinking/feeling.

What connection does my body have with his grandfather, and his own dormant dreams? Sometimes I imagine that when people speak to me, they can read my body, not as in body language, but they can see beyond the layers of clothes and skin to the stories inscribed on my body, as if viewing a movie. There are times when I go to the mirror and try to see beyond the face that looks back at me. I am trying to see the ancestral memory that my body houses, the national lineage, the stories that were told at the end of the day when folks gathered to rest and think of the day ahead. I close my eyes, and literally, the stories pop, and I move from one place to the next, dropping in on characters in the midst of their lives, and always I am welcomed, despite the most intimate of acts in which they might be engaged.

I am always invited to stay awhile, to listen, to observe, to advance whatever is taking place. So, recently, when I met this man, and he took my hand and immediately this story about this woman and him unfolded, I was startled, but not inexperienced with the channels that the story took. My body, I imagine, is like one of those luminous creatures whose skin glows, yet does not conceal its internal mechanism. My body glimmers, so bright at times that it can obscure the story even from me. I have to work that much harder to unearth it. Sometimes I am working with a transcript that has been tampered with or is so old the ink has faded, the writing is archaic and I have to really scrutinize to decipher its meaning, even more so its trajectory.

There is no chronological order to the codes my body houses. Some of the tales are contemporary and even younger than I am in age, but most are old, ancient, spanning several generations. It is no respecter of gender or class or geographic boundaries. The stories are grafted into my skin, written in the flow of veins, etched in the rope of muscles, dyed into body hair, imprinted on my finger-prints, caked in the wax in my ear, carried on my saliva, flowing in my blood, trapped in the brief gap between every inhalation and exhalation. They are present in my eyes, breathing among the follicles in my nostrils, clamouring for words on my tongue, forever alive, demanding and insistent as the ocean waves.

And what I have come to realize is that it is not the characters, these people who are calling me, but the very act of writing that calls, the need to make something up, the need to spin a tale, the insatiable need to create something from nothing, to dive into the core of my body and reach and pull until I have this to share.

The writing usurps my body for its own use, sees it as if it were a sheet of paper on which great details are printed. The writing is really the ringleader; it discerns the need to write out of a history that is longer than the tradition to which it belongs. Therefore the writing taps into my familial and cultural lineage, culling frag-ments, aborted or dormant dreams, snatches of anecdotes, re-visioning and rewriting the story that was never recorded or was ignored because it was not deemed worthy or grand enough – too ordinarily human. My body knows the language, the sound and nuances of the words needed to say what must be said; it knows the landscape upon which to place the characters; more impor-tantly, it knows the emotional range and depth from which these people speak. My body is not concerned with plot, but rather the people who move the plot – the quality of their lives, the amber strings of their memory, the zig-zag weave of their forgetfulness, the turgid incline of their pride, the putrid hand of their spiteful-ness, the grandiose lips of their laughter and hope. My body is endless realms, coded and complex, yet opaque and translucent, a giddying merry-go-round, speeding into a crash, unless I write. I write and the spinning stops. I write and the code is rendered decipherable, I write and my body eases – the tension dissipates, the world seems clear and all is light again. I write and my body is integrated, united, floating into a wholeness in the jungle of tales.

WHO I READ THEN, WHO I READ NOW
(Thanks, Al Young)

The question gets asked and asked again. All the time – a desire by students and readers to find the genesis of a poet's influence, as if knowing who I read will lead them to the miracle and madness that is language.

There is never enough time to tell them that it is more than who I read that feeds my work; it is my attention to life's details; it is *who* has influenced me as I was growing up and how their being stained me; and it is social issues that continue to pull me – these are still the greatest influences on my poetry, on what I write about. Often the poetry that most moves me is not in a book, but on the roadside, in a café or restaurant and comes out of the mouths of those who do not even recognize it is poetry.

Sometimes, the poetry is the sunset, the shimmer of the sun on flowers in summer – the sheer splendidness of the colours, the waltz of the breeze, the startled or contented look of a domestic animal doing an ordinary act. This is where the poetry lives and these are the kind of images that impact on and feed what I write. But there are poets who also help the work along.

Some of the newer members of my poetry family include Khaled Mattawa (Libya) Marilyn Nelson (African American) Claudia Rankine (Jamaica) Czeslaw Milosz (Poland), Joseph Hanzlik (Czech).

The elders, who were there from the beginning, before I even had an idea what I was doing included:

Pablo Neruda (Chile) Khalil Gibran (Lebanon) & Rumi (Persia/Afghanistan), Kamau Brathwaite (Barbados), Sonia Sanchez, Jayne Cortez, Langston Hughes, Countee Cullen, Margaret Walker, Henry Dumas, Lucille Clifton, Robert Hayden, Sterling Brown and Paul Laurence Dunbar (all African-Americans); Claude McKay & Louise Bennett (Jamaica) Aimé Césaire (Martinique), Audre Lorde (Caribbean/USA) Leon Damas (French Guiana), René Depestre (Haiti), David Diop (Senegal), Nicholás Guillén (Cuba), Octavio Paz (Mexico), Garcia Lorca (Spain) and Dennis Brutus (South Africa).

When I moved to California at the end of 1979, I discovered

Bob Kaufman and Kenneth Patchen. It was there that I came to love e.e.cummings, Ezra Pound, Denise Levertov and Edgar Allen Poe.

As a girl in Jamaica, my favourite poets were Henry Wadsworth Longfellow and Lord Byron.

The list of fiction writers would be extensive, but a few top ones who have had profound impact and who are constantly with me include: Peter Abrahams, Amos Tutuola, Nadine Gordimer, Jean Toomer, Buchi Emecheta, Octavia Butler, Willa Cather, Jane Austen, Camara Laye, Bessie Head, Chinua Achebe, Leslie Silko, Jacques Roumain, Louise Erdrich, Austin Clarke, Charles Chesnutt, Paule Marshall, Earl Lovelace, Alice Walker, Gabriel Garcia Marquez, Toni Morrison, Richard Wright, Toni Cade Bambara, C.L.R. James, Zora Neale Hurston, Roger Mais, Gloria Naylor, Ngugi Wa Thiong'o, Sembene Ousmane, James Baldwin, Edgar Mittelholzer, George Lamming, John Hearne, Samuel Selvon, Andrew Salkey, J. Edgar Wideman, Flora Nwapa, Rosa Guy and Wole Soyinka,

This is just a smattering of the fiction writers I read, as well as poets, and I am certain I have left out some important mentors.

I tell students and would-be or wanna-be writers that they will find their poet/writer guides when they are ready.

THERE IS ALWAYS A WAY:
GIFTED MY MOTHER'S MAXIMS

My mother lived her life without malice and never paused to lament over setbacks. Instead she forged ahead, finding alternatives, living her favourite motto, "Where there is a will there is a way." I had not known how much of my mother I had become until about seven years ago when I got divorced and found myself left with three children to support and raise. I was determined not to alter my lifestyle or deprive my children of opportunities. Whenever I felt overcome by bills or fatigue, I would say to myself, "Where there is a will there is a way" and doors would open for my children and I. My mother's proverbs were my mantras.

"There is more than one way to skin a cat," my mother hissed, depressing the accelerator and the car sped down the two-lane street as if it was the only vehicle on the narrow road. Both my mother's hands grasped the steering wheel and she was leaning into it, her eyes straight ahead. I kept glancing up the road before us and at her. I held my breath, hoping I would not explode. I had never witnessed my mother so angry with her youngest brother, my favourite uncle. Their raised voices had arrested me in the backyard where I played with my infant cousins.

"What you mean, you can't do it today? I said I was going to ask someone else and you said no need to pay someone for what you could easily do."

"Chu, Cathy. It can wait till next week. I've to make a run."

Suddenly my mother's humming intruded on my recall of that altercation. She was humming a hymn, interspersed with a few words of the song; soon her voice was full, taking liberty with the tune, until she filled up all the space in the car. I stuck my head out the open window and breathed.

"Don't hang out that window," she warned, picking up the rhythm of the song with ease. I turned fully in my seat to look at her face. She was smiling, the same wide-teeth grin that made her face appear to glow and I knew she wasn't angry any more, not at Uncle Seymour, not at anyone. I joined her in singing, a song that marked the beginning of many mornings. My mother often sang me awake, her voice strong and persistent as the sun.

By the time we had gone through the song twice, my mother had slowed her speed, but only slightly, because she always drove fast, speeding past other cars.

"Where're we going, Mummy?" I felt it was now safe to ask as she was sitting relaxed in her seat.

"Miss Mac," she replied, glancing at me. I didn't ask her why we were going to her best friend when we had only planned to visit Uncle Seymour, where I had hoped to spend most of the afternoon, playing with my two young cousins. At nine years old, I knew from experience that my mother would only tell me what she felt I needed to know. She would not discuss the details of the quarrel between her younger brother and herself, except to refer to it as "grownup business". Still I felt the air light enough to broach the subject.

"Mummy, are we going back to Uncle Seymour?"

"No," she said flatly.

I kept quiet, hoping she would say more. She slowed and turned onto a familiar street. We were not far from Miss Mac's house, with its sprawling yard, way back from the street, five dogs, and numerous fruit trees. Tamarind was in season so undoubtedly Miss Mac would give me a large bag to pick enough to take home so Mummy could make tamarind-ball and the tart drink that I loved, while they talked without me eavesdropping, and her dogs sniffed at my feet and at the tamarind lying on the ground.

"Opie," my mother's gentle voice brought me back to the present. "Your uncle and I not seeing eye-to-eye now, but remember, there is always more than one way to skin a cat. He thinks because I needed his help, I have to be inconvenienced. No sir," Mummy ended flatly. I had heard that tone before. I had all too often witnessed my mother willing the wind to stop for her, and more often than not it paused and allowed her to accomplish some task. She was generous to a fault, fiercely independent, and did not take kindly to anyone who did not keep his or her word or promised a favour then reneged. I deduced that was what happened between her and Uncle Seymour, because I remembered him saying that if she came by his house Saturday afternoon, as we had done, he would go with her to get something.

That was why I had thought I would be spending the afternoon with my cousins and my uncle's dimpled wife, Trisha.

Mummy stopped in front of Miss Mac's gate and blew the horn. The gardener opened the gate and we drove down the long path, the dogs racing and barking at the car, then we turned left and parked just beyond the wide-columned steps leading to the expansive wraparound veranda. Miss Mac was rocking on the veranda, and even before the car stopped, she climbed down the stairs and opened my door. As I stepped out, she hugged me in her fleshy arms, burying my face in her bosom.

"Cathy, what a pleasant surprise," she said releasing me and turning to my mother. "Shush dogs, shush," she said slapping at the side of her leg and turning to the dogs who were still barking. She ordered them, "Go sit down, go," her voice sharp and she clapped her hands together. The five dogs paused, angled their heads, and then slowly walked off, wagging their tails.

"Cathy, I was just sitting down to a tall glass of homemade cherry juice, come and join me. It is such a hot day." Mummy and Miss Mac embraced, and then climbed the five steps leading to the veranda. I followed at their heels. "Opal, you go in the kitchen and help yourself to two raisin cookies that I just made, and bring two glasses."

Before I was halfway through the door, I heard Miss Mac ask my mother, "So Cathy what brings you here this afternoon? I thought…" I dared not linger so I did not hear my mother's response.

As I had suspected, as soon as I was done with my cookies and juice, I was told to get a bag from the kitchen, and go and collect tamarinds to take home. The gardener was asked to pull some from the tall, tall branches. I wandered around the yard, playing more with the dogs than collecting tamarinds, and glancing every so often at the veranda to steal a look at my mother. I wondered how long we would be staying. I was curious to learn which cat my mother intended to skin and why. Perhaps that's why we had no cats. I felt sick just thinking about my mother skinning a cat. I convinced myself that she would not skin a cat just because she was mad with Uncle Seymour. Mummy was always using proverbs to teach me a lesson. Most times they had nothing to do with the things I thought, and half of them made no sense to me. Only last week, when I was sad about not getting the lead in the dance, Mummy said, "Time longer than rope." When she saw my puzzled face, because what does not getting the dance part have to do with time or rope, she hugged me and said, "Every dog has its day, every hour, its half-hour." I just shook my head and started to laugh. I knew in time, as always, "the light of day would dawn understanding," another of my mother's maxims that I was beginning to understand. About half an hour elapsed, the sun unrelenting, my shirt sticking to my back. By now I had filled up a big bag of tamarind and still many lined the ground.

Just as I decided to walk back to the shade of the veranda, a pickup truck stopped by the gate and blew its horn. I turned to see if I recognized the man driving, but I did not. Miss Mac did not call to me to open the gate, so I slumbered towards the veranda, dragging the large bag of tamarinds. Mummy and Miss Mac were walking swiftly towards me, and we met midway between the gate and the veranda.

"Be a good girl, and listen to Miss Mac," Mummy said, hugging me quickly and kissing me on the cheek. "I'm going to get something. Shouldn't be gone for more than an hour or so." Before I could collect my thoughts, she and Miss Mac were walking towards the gate and talking fast. I stood where they left me, feeling lost and alone. I saw Miss Mac talking to the man in the pickup truck, and then watched Mummy get in the front with the man and then they drove off. My heart dropped to my feet like a big coconut that I would never be able to pick up. I didn't know the man who Mummy drove off with, smiling. I had never seen him before. Immediately another of my mother's maxims popped in my head: "Not every skinned teeth is laughter." Maybe my mother wasn't really smiling. Maybe that man was taking her away from me.

It seemed like a very long time before Miss Mac stopped scolding the dogs and walked back to where I was rooted. I don't know if she saw my heart at my feet and felt sorry for me, but all I knew was that she was hugging me and she took the bag out of my hand.

170

"Is worry you worrying? Your mummy soon come back; she has to collect something, and my friend Mr. Taylor is helping her out. He has a daughter about your age. I should have told him to bring her to keep you company. But not to worry, you can help me shell these tamarinds, but first we will pick some cherries from the back. The trees are full," Miss Mac said, taking my hand.

I could feel my heart trying to pick itself up from off my feet.

"Come, Little Miss Cathy," Miss Mac said, pinching my cheeks, "Mummy soon come."

Usually I loved it when Miss Mac called me Little Miss Cathy. She never tired of saying I was the spitting image of my mother, hence her nickname for me. But now with my mother gone with that man, I wondered if she was calling me Miss Cathy because Mummy wasn't going to be coming back. I allowed Miss Mac to hold my hand and lead me to the back, but my feet dragged like a wet towel being pulled through the sand. All the while we picked cherries I kept chanting inside my head another of my mother's sayings, "After the rain, the sun is bound to come out." I understood this phrase and always shouted it after an afternoon summer shower as I ran back outside to finish my play. Mummy was the sun and that mean man, Mr. Taylor, was the rain that was keeping my mummy away.

After picking two large bags of cherries, Miss Mac and I went into the kitchen where we sat in the cool, taking off the brittle brown skin from the tamarinds, and de-seeding them in preparation to make tamarind juice. It seemed like forever since my mother had left. Miss Mac was telling me how she made tamarind juice, but that was not how Mummy made hers, so I looked at her and said, "Miss Mac, there is more than one way to cook chicken." She looked at me a little puzzled, as I often looked at Mummy when she said something like that, then she smiled and said, "There is sure more than one way, Little Miss Cathy."

I smiled and felt my heart crawling up my knee. Shortly after, my mother burst into the kitchen, smiling. I didn't even hear her enter. She handed me two small brown bags of warm peanuts that I loved. I threw my arms around her neck and squealed, "Mummy! You are back! Thank you," and opened the packet of peanuts, feeling my heart beating in my chest.

"So Cathy, you got it?"

"Yes. There was lots of traffic – that's why we took so long. Mr. Taylor made sure they wrapped it well so it wouldn't get scratched. He went home to have lunch. Said he would be back in a hour."

"Well Cathy, you must be hungry yourself. I was about to make some sandwiches," Miss Mac said, heading towards the breadbox.

"I brought us patties and coco-bread. I left them in the dining room. We just need some juice. Let me go and wash my hands."

"You must have read my mind," Miss Mac laughed. "I was just thinking I had a taste for patties. I will get plates and juice."

"Mummy, look how many tamarinds Miss Mac and I shelled. And we collect cherries, too, for us to take home."

"I see you have been working hard," my mother smiled, heading down the hallway towards the bathroom.

Mr. Taylor returned two hours later with a great big box in the back of his pickup and a little girl with small eyes, hair braided neatly in corn-rows and bouncing in the front of the pickup beside him. Mummy and I hugged and bade Miss Mac goodbye, got in our car, with Mr. Taylor following behind. Several times I had to remind my mother to slow down because I could not see the pickup behind us.

When we got to our house, Mr. Taylor said, "Miss Catherine, I see your foot don't spare the gas. You drive like a minibus driver. You dangerous on the road bad." He laughed and wiped his brow with his handkerchief.

My mother laughed and invited him into the house. Then turning to glance at me, she said seriously, "Manners and good breeding live in the same house." Then seeing my baffled look, she commanded, "Introduce yourself and offer her some juice," indicating Mr. Taylor's daughter who was still sitting in the truck.

"Mabel, you can come out and play, just mind yourself," Mr. Taylor said to his daughter as he stepped over the threshold.

The sun had set before Mr. Taylor and Mabel left. She and I had stayed outside the entire time, playing hopscotch and jumping rope. Our next-door neighbour, Mr. Williams, had come over to help Mr. Taylor lift the box from off his pickup truck, and I heard furniture being moved around, but I had no idea what my mother had bought. I didn't think our house could hold anything else, as every room was packed with large, dark mahogany furniture that I had to polish and dust, but at that time my concern was with play.

After we waved goodbye to Mr. Taylor and Mabel, my mother led me into the living room and right where the armchair and table used to be by the window, now stood a shiny rectangular structure, wider than the width of my outstretched arm and the height of just above my waist. I ran my finger over the top.

"It's very pretty, Mummy," I said, looking down at my reflection in the shiny surface. "What is it?"

"You like it?" she asked, reaching for a stack of 45" records. She fished through the stack, found what she was looking for, then raised the top of the rectangular box, and I saw the turntable. She put on the record and Fats Domino's voice blared and we danced around the room. We both clapped when the song ended. As my mother showed me how to stack the records, and tune the radio stations, I ran my hand over the word, Grundig, the brand of stereo-component that was new on the market.

That evening as we ate supper my mother said to me, "Just remember there is always a way, and always keep your word; don't make a promise if you think you won't be able to keep your word."

Two weeks later Uncle Seymour was back at our house with my cousins. My mother stacked the stereo with records, turned up the volume and we all danced around. My mother never mentioned the quarrel they had; it was as if it never happened. But just before Uncle Seymour left, as he hugged her, I heard him say, "Sorry Sis, I know how you are about promises."

"Your word must be as good as your spit," Mummy replied, hugging her brother and bidding him a safe drive home.

I value my mother and because I witnessed her keeping her word, even though sometimes at great personal inconvenience, I do not make promises lightly. I keep my word to my children, friends and colleagues, but mostly I keep my word to myself, honouring what's best in me. Like my mother, I believe one's word should be worth the saliva in their mouth.

THE EVIDENCE OF THINGS NOT SEEN
(2005)

As I was inching my way up to the front of the car-pool stop to pick up passengers, I wondered: What if I were to pick up a mass murderer, a rapist, a car-jacker, a crazy woman? It was possible. I didn't know anything about these people nor did they know me. The car before me drove up, stopped, and two perfect strangers, dressed in business attire, standing in a queue with others, stepped forth and got in. The car drove off and I took its place, making sure to brush off the crumbs from the seat from my children's eat-quickly-on-the-way-to-school breakfast so Mummy can make a mad-dash-to-the-city morning commute and I felt I should be apologizing to my car-poolers for the dirty mats. Two people approached my car, the first man got in the back and the second in the front. They said good morning. Dare I search their faces? Dare I ask them to produce IDs? I smiled, knowing it was already too late. All of us buckled up and I drove off, waiting for them to interrogate me: How long have you been driving? Have you had an accident lately? Who is your insurance company? The man in the back immediately opened his book and seemed to be reading; the man up front looked straight ahead. Silence. Not prone to unnecessary conversation, I enjoyed their quietness, going over in my head my workshop ideas.

It's not often that I have to drive to San Francisco from Oakland in the midst of the rush hours, but to my pleasant surprise, the traffic flowed and soon I entered the car-pool lane and sailed across the Bay Bridge in record time. I exited at Fremont, turned left onto Howard, and pulled up at the curb and my car-poolers disembarked with a polite, even reticent thank you. I wished them both a good day and headed on my way. Who ever thought of this system? Such a genius! Car-pooling is definitely the way to go if one has to engage in such a stressful daily journey.

But towards the end of the day, I paused to marvel at the incredible faith that was in operation in this system of sharing. Neither passenger asked to see my driver's license nor inquired about my driving history. They had no way of knowing that I was not a drunken, uninsured rascal motorist. (Of course, I *do* have a valid license and *am* insured.) I was awed at the manifestation of faith that, in myriad ways, we demonstrate daily in our lives.

For many, faith is connected to some religious dogma, and a belief in a power outside and superior to themselves. Yet without thinking most of us practice faith daily. The root of that word, *fides*, is Latin for trust. Each of us – those passengers whose faces I would not recognize, and who might very well not recognize me – was demonstrating trust in each other that morning. They trusted me to drive them safely across the bridge and I felt obligated, both nervous and extra cautious, to honour their trust. And I trusted that they were decent and would cause me no harm. This complete trust in people is replicated too many times throughout the day to tally. For example, my children's schools trust that I will pick them up after school, that I have given them the correct information to contact me, should my children become ill, or for whatever reason that the school might need to contact me. Likewise, my children trust that I will pick them up when school is out, rather than run off with the cute man from the car-pool, and catch the next plane to Jamaica. And if I were to do that, run off with the car-pool man, I/we would be operating on faith that the pilot is in fact who he says he is, and is not feeling suicidal that day and will get us to Jamaica safely.

"Belief without need of proof, confidence or dependence in a person." This is how faith is defined in the dictionary. It is sort of what love is, belief in the goodness of the person of our affection. I love him, therefore I trust him. My children love me so they have faith that I will continue to care for them and provide for their needs. Even when I get angry and shout at them for some infraction, they still believe that I will not shut the door and claim that I do not know them. My boss trusts that my degrees qualify me to teach, and that I will impart some knowledge and/or wisdom to the students who pay tuition. The students and their parents expect that they will learn to write, paint and draw and make things from being at this school. In this scenario we are all demonstrating faith based on the belief in the inherent goodness of people, and that each of us will do what we say. That's why the car-pool works. Some people want or need to drive and some just need to get to work without having to pay the fare, or be crowded in with a whole host of people on the bus or on the train. The system benefits everyone, including the environment, but our participation is an act of faith.

I offer this testimony to the few cynics who claim they don't believe in or trust anyone, and I dare them to identify a day in their life when they didn't exhibit trust in several people, most of whom they didn't know. I don't believe it's possible to live in this world without acting on faith, and I want to suggest that the kind of wanton faith that most of us practice daily would make a zealot look like a baby. Faith is woven into the very fabric of our lives. It is what keeps a society from disintegrating into total chaos. Faith is the evidence of things not seen – our inextricable dependence on each other. What then if we were to practice faith more consciously? How might such thoughtful practice enhance our lives? I am reminded of the maxim, "Faith can move mountains." I know my faith in things, in people, in a divine force has enabled me to accomplish things that initially seemed daunting, if not impossible. Perhaps faith is nothing more than sheer determination and willpower. Perhaps faith is really just a careful system of organization with checks in place. Perhaps faith is only the law of averages working in our favour. However you want to define it, the many faces of faith that I experience each day – and I am joyous that we unconsciously practice faith in each other – reinvigorate me. Thank you, car-pool riders.

A GOOD MAN TO LEAN ON, A FRIEND TO HANG WITH
(1997)

I am not sure how old I was when I realized that boys had more freedom than girls. They were less restricted, and allowed to explore beyond the boundaries of home. Girls were expected to be quiet, play with dolls and stay relatively neat. Boys could and often did walk around with their shirts off, prancing about the place. However, in my rural Jamaican community, such behaviour was forbidden to girls. I became a tomboy and was called such until the onset of adolescence. Because I was intrepid and declared to have gumption, traits not encouraged or observable in many girls, I played and engaged in many escapades with boys. When I was seven my best friend was William. With him I climbed trees, played marbles, and together we stole away from home and went swimming in the canals nearby. At ten I played police and thief with Charley and other boys, jumping off roofs, shooting birds and running through the woods nearby. I had an affinity with the boys and although I was often a year or two younger, I could beat them in fights – witness Michael's bloodied nose for tormenting my dog. Boys were my pals, my playmates and confidants. I felt very comfortable in their presence – one of the gang.

Throughout most of my life, except for a brief period during adolescence when it became awkward, I have always had male friends, men with whom I could explore aspects of myself in a safe, loving way. As a child, it was through playing and fighting with boys that I discovered my physical and strategic strengths and weaknesses. Observing and imitating boys in play, I was able to claim boldness, and through running and exploring the environment with them I discovered the magic in everyday living. Hanging out with boys opened up that part of my natural environment, with its myriad vegetation and wildlife, that would otherwise have been off limits to me. With boys I learned to pace myself and stick out my tongue at fear. With boys I was whole, not divided, acting by some arbitrary code of acceptable behaviour; all parts of me were connected and melded together in a cohesive, boundless energy. I had found men to be more adventurous, more spontaneous, more willing to go on a hunch, to run the gamut, to light both ends of the stick at the same time, to dare tomorrow and blast yesterday, to live simply in the here and now and not take on the consequences. This is of course a sweeping generalization, and I know many men who don't fit this profile and, conversely, numerous women who do. But these are the qualities that have attracted me to men.

However, it was Neville's ease, his jolly, comfortable way of being in the world, his genuine niceness, that drew me to him. Neville Hendricks is one of my best men friends and has been ever since we met in 1976. Although we no longer live in Jamaica, and he and his family live in Toronto and I and mine live in California, we have never lost contact, and whenever I need someone to talk to, he is the person who comes to mind. Only recently, while I was going through a separation that led to a divorce, Neville was the one person who I felt understood, without taking sides, voicing his support for whatever decision I arrived at, calling me frequently to check in. In some ways, going through this major change has rekindled our relationship, and I miss that he is so far away. If we were in close proximity, I would have been able to hang out with him, and the awful pain of this dissolution would have been eased in other ways. He would have enfolded me in his arms, dragged me places, made me laugh, kept me focused on the verdant mountain range, let me see sooner the rainbow after the storm.

Recently, trying to coordinate his visits to me on one of his business trips, I asked Neville if he remembered the circumstances of our meeting, and of course he did. We met at a one-week slide seminar in Jamaica to which our respective jobs had sent us and we immediately hit it off and became friends. Those first few years, there was hardly a week that went by when we didn't get together, taking drives, discovering our island, going dancing, just hanging and having fun with other friends, family, each other. We talked, we laughed, we walked, held hands, fooled around, ate watermelon, marvelled at the sunset and allowed the clear Caribbean ocean waves to splash over us. Our closeness caused his girlfriend, now his wife, some concern, doubting the platonic nature of our relationship. His other men friends questioned our friendship too, as did a few of my boyfriends/lovers. "Something must be gwane on between you two," a lover of mine insisted back then.

The notion that a man and woman can simply be friends is difficult for many to accept. Nonetheless, that's how Neville and I have been and remain even today. We have left our island home, married, had children (he has two, me three), and to his children I am an aunt, and to mine he is an uncle. Neville and I are family, and I consider him an integral and important part of my life. Yet Neville is not a brother, and I don't think I consider him as a brother. I have two brothers to whom, at various stages during my life, I was very close, so I know what it is to have a brother and Neville doesn't fit that category. Neville is like a left hand, a necessary part of my body that I can take for granted, yet still appreciate for its value. And he is more, a similar spirit, a navigator on the same road, a travel companion, someone to talk to without feeling the need to defend my boundaries and ideas, someone so comfortable it's okay to lean on him, fall asleep on him, leave my door and my heart open to and for him, secure in the knowledge that he will never abuse the privilege I have bestowed on him – and conversely. My experience has proven this to be the dividing line between a man who is a friend and one who is a lover.

With Neville and I, laughter is never far behind. Never a need for apology. During the first trimester of pregnancy with my first child, I went to visit Neville and his wife in Toronto. Naturally, we decided to go partying, to relive one of our common hobbies during our single days. Lee, his wife, was still not the partying type, so we decided to celebrate without her that night. However, it was short-lived because while I was very healthy and had no other pregnancy symptoms, I discovered I could not stay awake much beyond midnight. Reluctantly, we went home, and I had to live with him teasing me about making a liar of him. Neville had told his friends in Toronto that his good-good friend and partying partner was coming to visit and we would party the night away. Except, there I was falling asleep in the club, and by midnight had to be taken home. But it was okay, teasing and all; we laughed and reminisced about the *good old days* when we *could* party, even during the week, until 3 or 4 a.m. and get up and go to work refreshed the next morning. So much had changed, yet so much still remains fixed, unyielding.

I don't know why it is I can be such good friends with Neville, who doesn't necessarily share all the same philosophical or political outlooks as I, and yet not get into senseless arguments and fights as I do with others. I can't remember a time when I was spit angry with Neville or when we swore at each other or thought about putting an end to our friendship. I don't know what that would feel like. It's not a possibility I want to imagine or dwell on. Yet I was married to a man I loved and with whom I have children, and now that we are divorced I cannot entertain the idea of being his friend. How is that possible? What is it about Neville and I that has allowed us to remain friends for more than twenty years, even though we have not lived in close proximity for fifteen of those years. How is it that when the phone rings, and I pick it up and recognize his voice, our conversation sounds as if we are talking across town, as if we met only just yesterday, when in fact sometimes it's been several months? What is it that bonds us? How does he intuit my personal turbulence and always call me when I need his calm reassurance, knowing that he listens not only to my words, but the texture and breath of their meaning? We have a connection, and I love him dearly.

I value male friends; they help me to better understand lovers. They help me to better understand myself and my feelings. With a male friend there is attraction without sexual intercourse. There is intimacy and vulnerability without negative consequences. I can talk to Neville about very personal feelings and desires, fully confident that at some crucial moment down the road he won't use the information I divulged against me. It is not a trump card to pull out when pressed against the wall. I can be guileless, let my defences down, cry without worrying that I will be told my tears are a manipulative strategy. But mostly, Neville, my male friend, is a balance as well as an anchor: if he is alright then other men can't be so bad. In this my voyage into the fourth decade, I don't spend too much time pondering the whys, rather, I focus on the blessings, and this is what Neville is and has been in my life, a bounteous gift that has allowed me to reach deeper into my soul, discover strengths and abandon fears.

A BIRTHDAY CARD FROM MY FATHER

Today I receive a birthday card from my father and it puts a smile on my face. My father hasn't sent me a card in years. Nor have I sent him any. As I read the affections for a daughter printed in the card, my heart flutters, light as a butterfly. I turn the card over in my hand, admiring the deep blue sky of the landscape scene. I read the letter he includes, asking about my life, and I wonder what receiving a birthday card from my father means this year? I place it on my desk and glance at it, wishing it would reveal my father's thoughts.

He actually remembered my birthday, I say out loud, and rise from the chair and pace the floor in my office, and speak to the walls as if I'm addressing him.

Are you willing to see me as the woman I have become? Are you willing to treat me as an adult and respect my reservations as much as you are demanding that I respect yours? Are you able to call it a truce and allow us to enjoy the rest of the time and the life we have? I want us to find that place, and real soon, Daddy, I add.

I sit back down to write my father a letter of acknowledgement, but my pen stalls. I hesitate to write 'Dear Daddy'; it doesn't sound right in my head. I try 'Dear Orlando', and although that is his name, it doesn't have the emotional charge I want. How should I address him? What feels comfortable? I stand up and pace some more, ruminating. Why is this still so difficult for me? What answers don't I have that I want from him? Do I still need him to say: *I'm sorry I wasn't there for you all those years, but I loved you always*?

I tell myself again that I don't expect an apology from him, but a persistent voice says, "You deserve one. He owes it to himself, to you, to his ancestors and to the world to make peace with his adult children before he dies." The stubborn voice quiets and I chime: that's all I want, to make peace, for you to realize that I am no longer the little girl you left, who cried for her daddy. I am a woman. And if we are to have a relationship, it has to be as one adult to another, trying to find our way back to each other – to connect in the present moment.

I close my eyes and the past overtakes me as if it's doing a marathon race.

The most ineradicable and first 'memory' I have of my father comes from a story my mother told again and again as I was growing up.

I was only two years old, but I climbed to the peak of the guava tree in our front yard and I was unable to come down. You, my father, climbed as far as the branches would withstand your weight, then told me to jump. I jumped and you caught me in your arms.

The image of my father perched on a branch catching me in his arms, shimmers in my head. I want to know why he wasn't there to catch me all the other times I climbed too far and fell. Quickly, I brush aside that painful feeling, and continue on the happy path my memory wants to take me as I stare at the birthday card, with its image of a lone bird soaring in the sky.

★ ★ ★

"Daddy! Daddy!" I would shout, running to you.

You would catch me, raise me high up above your head, bring me close to your face for a kiss before setting me down on the ground.

"How is my little Mus-Mus?" you would ask, using your nickname for me. Then we, holding hands, would enter the house together. That was the evening ritual, when you came home from work.

You had a swagger in your gait and a smile so warm and dazzling it was contagious. I remember you walking without a shirt around the yard as you gardened. You loved growing things, and as you bent to the soil, pruning, planting, admiring your vegetables, perspiration laced the matted hair on your chest. An emerging potbelly hung over your shorts. I would follow at your heels, playing in the dirt with my stick shovel.

Once you put me to sit on your lap and allowed me to steer your car when I was not four years old. I almost steered it into the canal. I remember too that you wrecked your car while travelling to Kingston. The whisper is that you were drunk. I remember that when you came home from the hospital you had to be fed with a straw because you had injured your jaws as well as broken your leg – a miracle you survived. As I stood at the entrance of the room

182

watching my mother spoon-feed you, I whimpered, afraid to come close, my pain and fear trapped in my stomach, yours bound to you in the cast on your leg.

These are my memories of you that live sweet inside me; memories of a four-year-old girl. These images are indelible.

★ ★ ★

If there were angry words or screams, I don't remember them. What I remember is the stony silence that I did not understand. I remember terror, the day my mother left us without a word. No one spoke of her absence; all acted as if she had never been there.

Then three months later my mother returned, as silently as she had gone. She packed clothes for my sister and me in a hurry, issued urgent orders to load this or that piece of furniture onto the truck parked in our driveway. My sister and I were soon dressed, down to the ribbons in our hair. We got settled in the truck.

"Isn't Daddy coming?" I asked.

"No," was my mother's flat reply.

You stood on the veranda of our house. Your face was a frightened mask. I waved to you, but you did not wave back. My mother went to say something to you. She returned shortly, took her seat and pulled me onto her lap. The truck pulled off. I waved to you even after the truck had turned onto the main road. My arm soon felt weightless, so I draped it around my mother's neck. I was excited to be going on a trip, and glad for my mother's return... but anxious. I noticed tears trickling down my mother's face.

"Why you crying, mam? You miss you husband?" the truck driver asked my mother.

"No, he slapped my face," my mother said, drying her tears.

★ ★ ★

"Daddy come to get us!" my sister shouted, jumping up and down.

"Ah can't let you take them without them mother's permission, sar," the maid said, standing her ground, going to the telephone to call my mother at work. My sister ran into your arms. I stood back, playing with my skirt. You opened your arms and called me. I moved towards you. You ordered the maid to pack our clothes while you sat on the veranda, the two of us jumping in your lap. I heard the maid inside the house, making noises and mumbling to herself. You gave us candy from your pocket and tickled us. My sister and I tickled you.

Suddenly my mother rushed through the gate; she had a policeman with her. She ordered us to our room. We walked away, but we stopped at the living-room door.

"You will get them over my dead body!" my mother, ignoring us, said in no uncertain terms.

"They are my children too," you shouted.

Your voices were loud and clamorous, like glasses breaking on tiles. My sister and I were frightened; we hugged each other, tears streaming down our faces. Finally I heard the policeman telling you that you had to leave, that if you wanted you could go to court. I heard the gate open and close. The policeman told my mother if she had any more trouble to call. We came back into the room, my sister and I. My mother's entire body trembled as she took us into her arms.

★ ★ ★

"Daddy, please leave and not make a fuss," I prayed silently. Time had passed. I don't remember whether it was my sister's birthday or my own, but as always, my mother had thrown a big party with lots of children and grownups. You had come late, your hands empty. Now everyone was gone, it was dark, crickets sang, and mosquitoes were frantic in their search for blood. Yet you still sat on the veranda, having drunk too much, insisting, "You're still my wife." Mother alternately pleaded with you and ordered you to leave. "This is my house," she told you. "You don't pay rent here."

"You can't make me leave," you growled.

You stayed outside, locked out on the verandah in the dark. I was afraid Tutu the boogieman would take you off, never to be seen again.

★ ★ ★

For two weeks during the late summer, when the days were particularly long and hot, my sister and I used to spend time at your house, with Miss May and her daughter, Patsy. (I was grown before I learned that Miss May had been the cause of the divorce, and that Miss May's daughter, Patsy, two years my junior, was my half-sister.)

During those two weeks at your new home, my sister and I played outside almost the entire day, being left pretty much to ourselves. But when you came home from work in the evenings, when food was on the table and we sat to eat, you would scold us constantly about our table manners: Use your knife and fork. Get your elbows off the table. Don't touch that juice until your plate is clean – your voice, the relentless buzzing of a wasp. But I also remember how after dinner you fed Pretty Parrot, our pet, with its emerald green feathers. You taught him to say "Hello, how are you?" as he rocked from one leg to the other. Each day you cleaned his cage and gave him a small red pepper. Sometimes you would put Pretty Parrot to stand on my shoulder, or you showed me how to hold out my arm for him to stand on it. Dawn and I tried to teach him other words, and sometimes when he called to us, we were startled.

On Saturday afternoons you took us for drive-outings, just my sister and me. And very early Sunday mornings, when the air was still cool, you took us swimming at Gunboat's beach. The beach would be closed so early in the morning, but we would crawl through the barbed-wire fence. Even before my sister and I went into the water our teeth chattered. We'd wrap ourselves in large towels and refuse to swim, but you would grab us one at a time and take us on your back so far out into the sea that we could not see the shore. I would squeal, cling to your back and hug your neck tight. After a while, being way out there, the water would be soothing and warm. Still, I longed for dry land and prayed I wouldn't slip from your back and sink into the ocean. You were a marvel in the water, swift and slippery as an eel. By the time we went home, the sun would be out, prancing all over the place; the gate would be open and people would be coming in droves for their ritual Sunday at the beach. Once I asked you why we went so early, before anyone else got there. Smiling, you said, "The water is best when there is still a chill to it."

★ ★ ★

When your father died, my paternal grandfather, he left behind a wife who was younger than my mother, and a son five years younger than me. I was eight years old at the time. My mother, my sister and I arrived very late the night after he died. It was so dark I'm not sure how we got there. Relatives greeted us and inspected my sister and me, passed us from hand to hand and hugged us. My grandmother, your mother and grandpa's first wife, took charge of us. She said even though she was still angry with Grandpa, he was dead and gone so she came to bury him; and, with the rest of us, she stayed in what had used to be her house. You and Grandma took my sister and me into the room where Grandfather's body lay, covered with ice. It was customary in some parts of rural Jamaica, and probably still is, to keep the dead at home until burial. I asked you why Grandpa was covered with ice. You replied, "To keep him from rotting."

I kept on going into the room to peek at Grandpa and to see if he would get up. But he never did, not even when I took a handful of ice-mint from the sweetie jar on the counter, in the adjacent shop area. People remarked what a brave child I was, not being afraid of the dead.

I know Grandfather had been a big man in the little village. His house and adjacent shop, the only store in the village, were the only places other than the church that had electricity. For four days we waited for the arrival of relatives and friends from around the island and abroad. I saw very little of you during this time. But on the day Grandpa was to be buried, you came and snatched us from the yard where we were playing with the many cousins we had recently discovered. You ordered us to be quiet and led us into the small, dimly lit room where Grandpa was being prepared. It smelled like dirty, damp clothes in a bin. My mother was already there, with some men I did not know. Grandpa lay there, bloated and ashy. You washed my face and hands in a basin of water on the table next to Grandpa; then you washed my sister's. You told us that Grandpa would protect us. Next, you lifted me up and passed me over Grandpa's body, handed me to one of the men on the other side. As you did so you asked Grandpa to always protect and walk with me. You did the same with my sister. Mother took us from the room then, and we waited for what seemed like an eternity in the dark, still hallway. You came at last and took us back into the room, where we could see that in our absence Grandpa's body had been dressed in a suit. And you helped first me, then my sister, to put on one of Grandpa's socks. My sister and I held your hands as we walked the hundred yards to the church. When it was all over, we stood in the churchyard and watched dirt fill up the hole on top of Grandpa's coffin.

We left that same night, my mother, my sister, and I. I was asleep, so I didn't get to kiss you goodbye.

A few years later, Aunt Lyn, your sister, died. She never made it home from the airport after returning from America. (The talk was that she had worked herself to death there.) At her funeral, I remember thinking your face looked like a hard, dry coconut still in its shell; you seemed vexed with the world and I couldn't think of anything to say to make you laugh.

Finally, I remember a party at Nanny's, your mother's house, where you arrived very late with a woman. Although my mother looked beautiful in a shiny blue dress, neither of you spoke to each other. How could that be and you were married, I wondered. People were whispering about you at the party and I had to keep moving away so as not to hear what they were saying. My stomach kept tying up in knots and I had to press on it.

★ ★ ★

These are all the memories I have up until I was ten, not yet eleven years old. Then you disappeared from my life. No more telephone calls. No letters, no birthday cards, no presents. Nothing. Mother said she didn't know where you were, but that she'd heard you had moved to America. Grandma claimed she didn't know where you were, but Mother didn't believe her.

At first I would sit on the steps and listen for the postman's bicycle bell. When I heard it ringing, I ran to the gate and took the mail from him. There was never any letter with my name on it. You didn't write but I wrote to you when my playmates in the neighbourhood chanted:

"You don't have a daddy! You don't have a daddy!"

"Yes I do!" I shouted back, tears stinging my cheeks. I ran home, tore a page out of my exercise book and wrote:

> Dear Daddy:
>
> Please come and visit. My friends think I don't have a daddy, and I do. They are so stupid. Please come so I can introduce you to them. Once they meet you, they will know that I have a wonderful daddy.
>
> Your very best daughter, Mus-Mus

I even signed it with your nickname for me, but I never mailed it. I didn't know your address.

After a while, I no longer listened for the postman, but every so often I wondered where you were, what you were doing, whether you missed me? I knew you had to be hurt not to come to my birthday party or send me a card. Then I thought you must be angry with me for choosing to live with Mummy instead of you. That's why you didn't come to see me any more. That's why you didn't write. I tucked you away, but would pull you out every so often. When I had my first dance performance I sent you an invitation:

> Dear Daddy:
>
> You will be so proud of me. Finally I will be dancing at the Little Theatre. My dance teacher, Miss Campbell, is very strict, but she says we are ready to show off. The costumes are colourful, and we even get to wear make-up. I'll be dancing Friday, Saturday and Sunday evening. Come to any of the shows.
>
> Love your dancing daughter, Opal

Each night before show-time, I peeped out from behind the curtain to try and find you in the audience.

> Dear Daddy:
>
> Why didn't you wait around after the show? I took off my costume hastily and ran out to greet you, but you always left before I came out. I didn't mean to take so long to change my costume, Daddy.

Then my life began changing quickly. At thirteen, although Mummy said I was too young to have a boyfriend, this cute boy liked me and I knew you would understand that I was not too young.

Dear Daddy:

Can Devon please be my boyfriend? He is very nice and plays soccer. His favourite subject in school is Chemistry. He might be a chemist like you when he grows up. I like him a lot and everyone says how mature I am. Please tell Mummy that I am old enough to have a boyfriend.

Your loving daughter,

Opal

Devon was never my boyfriend, and several months later, I saw him after a soccer match holding hands with and smiling in the face of another girl. I walked ahead of my friends so they wouldn't see my tears.

You never replied to any of my letters. You never called. You never visited. You never sent birthday cards. You were not present at most of the major or minor events in my life, and I needed you, wanted reassurance that you loved me. I ached to know where you were. It hurt. And I cried. Some days, I sat under the ackee tree and cried from missing you. Some mornings I woke up, and realized I was crying in my sleep from dreaming about you.

Dear Daddy:

This is an SOS. Where are you? Please come and visit. I just need to see you. I feel so alone as if no one understands me, but I know that you would. Come soon.

Your needy daughter with love,

Opal

I didn't write you after that, and I convinced myself that I didn't have a daddy after all, and that was okay. You were not dead, just erased, your place covered over with stones like the ones we piled to mark where we buried my dog, Brownie.

★ ★ ★

Seven years later my mother took us to New York to go to college. Grandma (who had migrated four years earlier with my deceased aunt's girls) would only say that you were somewhere in New York, but would not give us your address or phone number. You did not seek out or contact us, though I secretly believed I would run into you on the street or that you would track me down, ask for my forgiveness and say how you had been looking for me. You would call me Mus-Mus and tell me how much you had missed me. But five years in New York went by and I never once heard from you, until a few weeks after my college graduation.

I arrived home, and Mummy casually said, "There is a letter on the bookcase addressed to you and Dawn from your father."

I think I paused. I am sure I must have made some response. I remember taking up the letter and looking to make sure it was indeed addressed to me. I saw your return name and address and I kissed my teeth and placed the letter right back on the bookcase.

"It's too late," I said as I headed up the stairs for my room.

My sister read the letter as soon as she came home. I asked her what you said. She said I should read it myself. I kissed my teeth again and walked out of the room. A few days later, alone at home, the letter still on the bookcase, I took out the pages and read it. I wish I could remember exactly what it said, but I don't. I do know it was a "Dear Daughters" letter, as if we had been in contact with you all along, as if you hadn't just dropped out of our life without a word. I threw it in the trash, but when my sister came home, she asked if I had read your letter, and when I said I had and had thrown it away, she fished it out. She might still have it for all I know.

At my mother's encouragement, after my sister called and spoke with you, we took the long train ride to White Plains, New York and visited you. When we got off the train and I saw you there, you looked the same, and you didn't. It felt like time stopped when you took us back to your house. Your wife hugged us like long-lost and now returned daughters, then told us to hug our sister, her daughter Patsy, now grown, the same little girl we used to play with, just a year and a half younger than me. That meant she was born while you were still married to my mother, while you lived as husband and wife. All this time and I didn't know that she was my sister. My tongue lay heavy in my mouth and I felt as if I was holding in my stomach. I don't remember what we talked about, but it was all centred around the present and light as a lone leaf floating from a tree. I visited you once more before I returned home to Jamaica. I promised I would write and

I did, the kind of vapid, here-is-what-I-am-doing obligatory letter every three months. I kept hoping that you would fill in the blanks about your absence, but you never did.

★ ★ ★

Four years later I had moved to California. After putting an abrupt end to several fairly good relationships for reasons that I did not understand, I decided to try therapy. During one session, I recalled that last visit to you. When my sister and I emerged from the train station on that Sunday afternoon four years earlier, you embraced and kissed us and called me by my pet-name, "Mus-Mus". Immediately, I was a little girl again, longing for my daddy. I said none of the things I had rehearsed in my head. I had no accusations for you, didn't ask you to explain why you had left us without telling us, or whether you had missed us and thought about us. I said nothing. We all acted as if there had never been a separation, never a rupture. Yet I do remember feeling cheated when you said how proud you were of the two of us for having finished college. I bit my lip, and I thought, "Convenient of you to surface now, when we no longer need anything from you." And when I was getting married, I mailed you an invitation. You wrote to congratulate me, said you didn't like travelling and sent money for a wedding present.

My therapist suggested that my penchant for ending relationships might have stemmed from an impulse to leave men before they abandoned me, as I believed you had done.

Some years into my marriage I wrote to you. I addressed you by your first name and asked all those questions I had wanted to ask four years before. I did this in part prompted by my relationship to my father-in-law, Vinnie. (Later, when my second child was born and my husband and I went visiting relatives back east, we came to meet you. You prepared a nice meal for us and we had a pleasant dinner. But after we left I remarked to my husband that I felt closer to his father, as a daughter, than I did to you.)

I wrote:

> Dear Orlando:
> In the most ideal time and place that lives in my imagination, you and I grew up together. You watched me

191

mature; I witnessed you age. We enjoyed a close, loving relationship. I would tell you about the men I fancied, the man I would marry, and you would advise. Mostly, you encouraged me to be myself, to follow my dreams relentlessly and to live with integrity and honesty, always.

And if like now, we lived in separate states, we would call each other weekly. We would write to each other regularly, and you would tell me stories about your life as a boy and then as a young man. My head would be full of you, and I would carry you around in my heart, always. We would visit yearly, and while my children run around and mess up your neat home or fumble through your old, mildewed photo albums, you and I would talk over a cup of tea or stroll through your garden. Our arms would be hooked, and we would talk and laugh and lean on each other, happy that we are father and daughter.

Peace,
Opal

You replied, but ignored all my questions, the whole substance of my correspondence, choosing instead to focus on the manner in which I had addressed you. You admonished me never again to address you by your first name, but to call you "Daddy", or you would refrain from communicating with me. This response sent me into a rage. Had you been standing close to me, I could have ripped your heart out. I swore at you, and promised myself I'd never write to you again.

But after a few years I relented. I wrote again, and again you refused to answer questions.

To this day, you still have not answered the questions that matter to me, even though we stay in touch. The years have passed, and having children of my own has helped me to find a comfortable space for the old hurts, and to make space for love and sharing. Life with a sensitive husband helped me to grow beyond my fears and to stop torturing myself about the things I could not change. But more even than that, the wonderful open, adult relationship I enjoyed with Vinnie, my husband's father, contributed to the healing of the old wounds. Vinnie, who is your age, treated me as an adult. We talked and shared private feelings. I learned that I could not seek answers and love in places where none are to be found, no more than I could demand that you acted in any certain way.

My children are very close to their other grandparents, including my mother who comes and spends time with us, and often we go and visit her during the Christmas holidays. I have a family wall and a picture of you is displayed there along with my mother and other relatives. One day my youngest, far too precocious for her age, asked me how come she has never met my father and why I didn't call and talk to him like I did her other grandfather. I simply told her that we weren't that close, and promised that I would take her to visit you. Later that day, when I had a moment to myself, I reflected on my daughter's words, and felt that I was depriving both her and you from having a relationship, and I wanted to bridge that gap. I imagined my children and I visiting you and I imagined how afterwards I would compose this letter.

Dear Daddy:

I am so grateful you are in my life, and that you are my father. Words cannot give flavour to the joy I felt seeing you with your grandchildren, my children, and how much my youngest is like you. I don't think I had known that before our recent visit.

I so enjoyed the time I got to spend with you and the candid talks we had.

I am so thankful that you accept me for who I am, and that you listened to me and really heard me. I am pleased that you are able and willing to share so much of your life as a gift with me. We are all the wealthier for sharing so abundantly with each other.

I have taken your advice about the tomatoes, and mine are already looking better. Thanks too for the gentle way you told me to slow down and not take on the world all at once. I want you to know that I really heard your love and worry for me. I am going to make some major changes because I don't want to take off years from your life from worrying about me.

Your grandchildren really enjoyed the time they spent with you. They especially loved the stories you told them about your father, and how he came to be the owner of a store. I hadn't heard that story before so thanks for sharing it with us.

Daddy, I wish you and I could travel to Jamaica and visit your father's land, and go to his grave and thank him for helping to bring you into the world. Then you could show me the place where you grew up and point out the trees you climbed and the rivers you swam and the people you knew and where they lived. I wish all of us could take a trip back there, stop at Gun Boat Beach, take a swim and let the soothing salt water refresh us. We would visit your mother's and sister's graves too, and mourn and celebrate their lives. Maybe we could even get another parrot like the one we had and call him Pretty Parrot 2.

Daddy, I am glad you are proud of me, and I want you to know how important it was to have you say that to my face, kiss my cheeks, hold my hands, and call me your little, grownup girl.

I love you Daddy. I love you, and daily I thank the divine creator that you joined with my mother to have me.

All my love, Daddy. I'll talk with you soon.

Walk good,

Your darling daughter, Opal

P.S. By the way, Daddy, what is your favourite colour and food? That little spitfire granddaughter of yours wants to know all about you, and I do too. I am so sorry that I don't know those things about you, but when you tell me, I will never forget.

That was what I always wanted. Later, when my husband, two older children and I went to White Plains so you could meet them, seeing you again after so many years made me realize that you were becoming an old man. Five years ago when you were diagnosed with glaucoma, I had thought then, ungenerously,

"Justice for your neglect, old man. Maybe now, like Oedipus, you will be able to see the errors of your ways." But you are not a Greek tragic-hero. You remain obdurate, in many ways a stranger. But I felt lucky to have the fond as well as painful memories of you. I no longer look to you for the answers to my questions. I have forgiven you your absence in my life. And since I no longer wish you dead, I send you birthday cards.

★ ★ ★

The phone rings and I am brought back to the present. I glance at the card on my desk. I decide it is time to visit you and bring my youngest to meet you.

DINNER AT MY FATHER'S HOUSE
(December 2000)

I was in New York on business so took the opportunity to call my father with the intention of visiting him. As I hoped, he was happy to hear from me and invited me to dinner. I accepted eagerly, determined once and for all to ask him why he had not contacted me for ten years, from when I was ten years old to twenty. I wanted to have a heart-to-heart, come-clean-once-and-for-all talk with my father. I realized that those years were still splattered with pain and it was way past time to heal my feelings of abandonment and truly forgive the past.

I arrived at my father's suburban home an hour later than I said, as my ride was delayed. We embraced, tentatively, and my father invited my friend and I into the living room, then almost immediately brought us drinks and cookies. Although my friend was only dropping me off, he accepted, and we sat around, drinking and small-talking. I observed my father keenly, as if seeing him for the first time. He was a well-preserved man, short, elegant yet simple. I noticed that there was an orderliness about him and that he carried himself with decorum, as if he knew he was important. I smiled, thinking about my own haughtiness, which I had always assumed I got from my mother. Although my father had lost sight in one eye to glaucoma, he moved purposefully, like a man who is about doing things. He had aged well, hardly any gray, only a few wrinkles, but I realized that he was much smaller than the image of him that is imprinted in my head from childhood. Anxious for answers, I scanned the living room that hadn't changed much since my first visit in summer 1975, plastic on the sofa. For whom was he preserving this furniture?

After an acceptable time, politeness satisfied, my friend begged off with another appointment. Once he left, my father seated me at the dining table that was already set and announced that dinner had been waiting. He declined my offer to help, insisted that I sit and relax as he stacked three albums on the record player before he began putting the various dishes on the table, an enormous spread, which he had prepared himself. Old ballads that I hadn't heard since I was a child issued from the record player. I asked him about the titles of some of the cuts as he walked to and from the kitchen with food and juice, the lyrics springing forth from the recesses of my memory.

Over a delicious meal of baked turkey, rice, salad, and steamed carrots and pumpkin, we small-talked. I asked about Patsy, this sister who still doesn't feel like a sister, and whose whereabouts always seemed a mystery. I inquired about cousins, his nieces, with whom I had been close before the family splintered, moving to the USA. I collected details about their marriages, children and grand-children, and got their recent addresses. As my father cleared the table and washed dishes, again declining my offer to help, I marvelled over his record collection. No CDs in this batch. Nothing more recent than the early 80s. Time seemed frozen here, and I wondered if this was an indication of where his memory lay.

After my father was through with the kitchen, I invited him to join me at the table so we could talk. My underarms immedi-ately got sweaty. I couldn't help but feel like a little girl petitioning her father for some favour. I turned over the rehearsed phrases in my head, but the words came out direct:

"Why didn't you contact us for ten years?" I asked, looking at him keenly.

"There was never a moment or a day that I didn't love and think about you and Dawn," he began almost immediately, as if he had been waiting to tell me this.

"But you never wrote. Never sent us birthday cards or any-thing," I rejoined on the heels of his words.

He appeared to reflect on my accusations. I hated how I was feeling, like the little girl wanting her father. But I knew I had to be done with this part of my life, this need to have the past filled in – a puzzle with missing pieces. I still wanted and desperately needed to hear him offer some kind of explanation.

"When I first came to America, I wasn't straight, wasn't legal. Things weren't easy for a long time..."

I knew that story well, unrecorded as it was. It is the story of countless people from the West Indies who lost children, wives, husbands, parents, and each other in the process of getting a Green Card. I hadn't imagined my father, educated, a chemist, respected back home in Jamaica, as one of many immigrants trying to find a footing. I listened closely as he related his story, but after a while it didn't matter any more. In that moment, hearing his explanation, I chided myself about why I had made such a big deal about those lost years for so long. But the truth was, I needed to hear him say it; I had to have my father admit, confess that he loved me even though he never contacted me for all those years.

After he was through with his explanation, my father invited me upstairs to his study.

As I entered, I was confronted with several pictures of myself at various stages and at different ages. Pictures of my sister and I and our children filled the walls, along with a copy of some writing award I received. The maxim, "Action speaks louder than words," had weight that evening, because in that moment, if I ever doubted that my father loved me, seeing images of myself on his wall, in his private and cherished space, dispelled all doubts. And although our conversation felt like two long-lost friends meeting up again, somewhat unsure about how personal to get with each other, I was happy and relieved. I had found my way back to my father; I was not a forsaken little girl any more.

We pored through his photo albums, and he pointed out relatives whose names I had forgotten or perhaps had never known. I saw pictures of my father as a young man that I didn't ever remember seeing, and I certainly didn't remember ever knowing that he was a sprinter in high school. At my request, he graciously loaned me some of the pictures to copy for my own album, especially those of my deceased grandfather and grand-mother when they were young, and a few pictures of my sister and I when we were five and three years old, respectively.

When I left close to 10 p.m. that night, well after my father's normal 8:30 p.m. bedtime, I knew I had finally shed the past and it could no longer keep me in bondage. "Good night, Daddy," I said as I embraced him goodbye. I felt light and was happy that I was my father's daughter. That night, just before I went to bed, for the first time that I could remember as an adult, I gave thanks for my father connecting with my mother to make me. I vowed, no matter what, to always be in contact with him, not out of any sense of obligation, but because I wanted us to be in each other's lives.

This past summer, I took my children to meet my father. My oldest daughter had met him a few times, and so had my son, as an infant, but my youngest, then ten years old, had never met him. They had a short visit, but he showed them his garden, the pumpkins and tomatoes he grew and the well-tended yard. In the warm August afternoon, they sat outside, sipping juice, eating biscuits and talking. They brought their cameras and eagerly took lots of pictures, which they now cherish. Like me, my children were impressed with their grandfather's study, walls of photographs, some of themselves, some of me they had never seen. They too came to realize that even though they did not see or talk to their grandfather, they meant something to him. He even showed them some of the cards and notes they had sent him over the years. My son was duly impressed and told me that we needed to visit Grandpa more often. I assured him that we would.

When we left my father's house after a satisfying visit, I felt as if I had fulfilled two important promises. The first to my youngest child, taking her to meet her grandfather; and the second, to myself and my father – at last, I had allowed the ebb of the sea to wash the debris of the past into the belly of the ocean.

We live on opposite coasts, too far to visit often and try to bridge those gaps – so much about me he doesn't know and never will, and vice versa. However, we are living in the present, certain of each other's love. All my nagging questions have disappeared, replaced with a quiet appreciation of how fortunate I am to have both parents alive and to be in touch with both. Orlando is my father and I am happy we reconciled the past. I call him Daddy, although it feels new coming from my mouth. I respect and honour his desire for me to address him as that.

I vow to share as much of my life with my father as he is willing to share, and to tell my children all the stories I remember of him. I am delighted that they now know their grandfather and have a real person to go with the pictures. They write and call him, and daily learn more about their long-denied maternal grandfather.

I am enormously glad that time has been so kind to my father and I, and daily I offer blessings to the universe for reuniting us, forever father and daughter.

BOTH FEET WET AND ARMS
WAVING IN THE AIR
(2004)

I never imagined that I would become a cradle robber, that I would lust after young men, that I would have such erotic fantasies, that I would become a dirty old woman. My teenage daughter first identified my new preoccupation and said, "Mummy I think you are going through a mid-life crisis. You can't be liking guys that I'm almost old enough to date."

I was discovered! What to do but admit, confess my obsession and wallow in it. I made no apologies. I was not, am not ashamed. Nothing gives me a better high than man-watching, and, damn! there are so many beautiful chocolate, muscle-tight young men under the age of thirty. They are everywhere I look. I flash them bold smiles. Openly tell them they are gorgeous. Flirt. Run my hand over their strong bodies. Swish my ass and tease. I didn't skip a beat when three years ago, then forty-five, I was propositioned by a twenty-nine-year-old who asked, "So how old are you? About thirty-five?" I smiled demurely and seduced him to my bed. It was a delicious three-month fling.

By the time I turned forty-three I knew I was having fully-bloomed mid-life issues. The grey hairs were depressing me so I sought colouring, something I had sworn I would never do. Although I am not so bothered by the greys now, I still cover them over.

I knew I was a victim of my heterosexual persuasion, that being a divorcee with twenty extra pounds didn't help and that I lived in California, where it seemed most of the eligible Black men (my first preference) were predisposed to anything other than Black women. I was having a hard time. I didn't dress sexy, with my loose-fitting African garb, my natural hair and plenty, take-no-victim-no-time-for-any-games attitude. Talk right or don't even waste my time. Men over forty bored me. They were tired like the husband I had gotten rid of; they lacked excitement and sponta-neity and thought renting a videotape was high fun, an acceptable way to spend a Saturday night. Yet this is not true for all the men in this age group. There are those who still have verve, usually those men who are working at something they love and not waiting for that distant time when they retire to live their dream.

I was feeling free; my children were finally old enough for me to leave them alone, without having to cart them everywhere with me. I was feeling energetic, as if I were twenty, though I didn't want to be back there mentally. I just wanted my sexy, twenty-year-old body back. I would glance at young women with their slender bodies, fresh, youthful, expectant faces and was forced to admit to myself there was a trace of envy. I became embarrassed to look at them knowing the inevitable comparison that would follow. Nor could I look at pictures of myself when I was in my twenties, because no matter how much I told myself I hadn't aged, or that I looked good for my age, which I do, I would see my youthful face in those pictures, and I would know. Often I couldn't even recognize myself. Was that the same me? Where did that me disappear? Had I been so buried with having children and a marriage that she left me without me realizing it? It was such a shock. So painful. Then I began to affirm that I was beautiful as I am and in the perfect place and time, and gradually I began to re-love myself as I am now – forty-eight and blessedly fine and full of life.

Now when young men flirt with me, I tell them my age and take it from there; but my desire for them has not diminished. They inspire me. Many days I am only able to complete running around the lake by trailing after one of those young men speeding ahead, thighs like steel, which I imagine are wrapped around me. I complete my run, a feat I would never have been able to accomplish without such lustful inspiration. But mid-life is not all about sex and lust, just a major part. Perhaps it is true about women in their forties being highly suited for men in their late twenties or early thirties. The sex is definitely charged and dancing is sensuous. I truly love this phase of my life. I love doing just what I please. Love going against the grain and being scolded by my children who are more critical than my mother ever was: "Where are you going, Mummy? Who's that man? I don't think you should wear that." They are worse than the police.

I am settling into being a sexy diva with a cayenne pepper tongue. I look around me and many of my friends are already fifty and they are so fine and vibrant, I am honoured to be in a community of sisters who are globetrotters, self-assured women with places to go, things to do and lots to say. We are still the generation that believes in making a contribution to our community, but no longer at the cost of our own health and wellbeing. The other morning I called a sister-friend around 9:30 a.m. She answered the phone leisurely and told me she was luxuriating in her bed, and would get up when she felt like it. I was right there with her. I seldom feel the need to prove myself – as the saying goes, been there, done that! Snap finger, 180 degree turn. See you! I more easily say no without feeling I have to be there for everyone. Now, first and foremost I have to be there for me. I am very impatient with people wasting my time, having nothing to share but petty gossip. I am rediscovering and enjoying activities I indulged in my youth like dancing. I am taking two dance classes, Afro-Haitian and Salsa. I do yoga and meditate daily. I go for leisurely walks three times a week. I have given up wearing a watch and rushing around like a madwoman, though I am almost never late any more. I feel good to be alive in this moment and at this time. Now I get the meaning of good living, really working at what you enjoy and being grateful. Gratitude becomes me.

I enjoy silence, those not-long-enough periods when my children are at their father's and I have the house all to myself. What ecstasy! What a blessing! I never turn on the TV or radio. I bask in the silence. I enjoy candlelit baths. I turn off my phone and I love myself in ways I never knew how to when I was in my twenties. This is what approaching fifty means: not needing anyone to have a good time. I love going to the movies by myself, strolling about, people-watching. I am my own best company. Sure, sometimes I crave the company of a nice man, intimacy, but lots of time I am just fine by myself. I am concerned about the menopause, but not unduly. Recently my periods have been very painful and I experience mood swings a few days before the onset of my menses, something that never happened before, but I have my children trained. Now all I have to say is: it's that time of the month and they fall into place. My son in particular is wonderful. I hope he will make some woman happy. He suggests that I go to bed and offers to fix me something to eat. He always listens because he knows if he doesn't, I am likely to go off on one of my hollering sessions with only the slightest provocation. So now I know when my period is due, I need more rest, and I take it. I don't stress about having to cook dinner, or attend a meeting or any of the myriad things I used to insist on doing. Daily, I am learning more and more how to listen to my body, to applaud it for sustaining me, for bearing three beautiful children and for giving me enormous pleasure.

Recently, I have been reflecting on mortality. I lost three good friends in their mid-fifties to cancer a few years ago. I think about caring for parents, both in their seventies, as they advance in age. I think about my own mortality and what personal as well as professional legacies I want to leave behind, and how I can forge ahead to build those foundations. I am now thinking about where I want to retire, who I want to share the rest of my life with, what quality of life I want to enjoy. I am more sensitive to others' feelings, but I do not take on other people's issues. I am not trying to change anyone, not even my children. I see their innate personalities and try to adjust as best as I can to who and what they are. I am more spiritually connected than I have been since I was thirteen years old and left the church. I have found a religion, Science of Mind, that speaks a language that feels like mother-tongue and is intelligent and compassionate. I am working at ridding myself of judgement. I am in love with all aspects of life. So many simple everyday ordinary things make me smile and my heart flutter: waking to the birds chirping; noticing the first apple bulb on the tree; observing two complete strangers expressing love; giving a smile as I walk by and having it returned to me; talks with my teenage daughter and her friends; dinner with my children; breakfast date with a girlfriend during the middle of the week; sitting on a park bench in reverie.

I am so glad I have had this opportunity to be single at this age and to learn to discover, appreciate and truly love myself again. I see some women who are younger than I am and they seem so old. They have allowed life to beat them to the ground. They have given up on themselves. They are bereft of hope. They no longer know what it is to dream. They are preoccupied with things. But there is hope for such women. They just need to look inside themselves, find their art and express themselves fully in the world.

I never thought I would live so long, that I would reach the point when there was nothing I wanted or needed, but the truth is I have no need for any more material things, not even jewellery, which I love. I tell my children and friends all my needs and wants are met. So for birthdays and holidays, if they insist on giving me a present they know the only things I want are gift certificates for massages, manicures and pedicures, to spas and for facials.

Life is good and very good, but I still have not grown comfortable with the greys… I am inching there. My knees sometimes ache, but I am stretching and exercising them. I fully intend to continue kicking up my heels, in more ways than one, if you get my drift. I plan to continue to enjoy younger men flirting with me and thinking me ten years younger than I am. I am honoured that women who meet me are surprised when I tell them my age. I thank the good genes, the healthy diet, but mostly a positive attitude and my gusto for life and all it has to offer.

Don't look for me on dry land, I am wading in the ocean of life, feet wet and arms waving for others to join me.

TRIBUTES

A TELLER OF TALL TALES:
IN MEMORY OF TONI CADE BAMBARA
(1996)

I first met Toni Cade through her short story collection, *Gorilla, My Love* (1960), which I taught in my freshman composition class at San Francisco State University. It remains one of my favourite collections because Bambara's characters are spunky survivors and their voices lift off the page. I had the pleasure of meeting Toni Cade in 1984 when I advocated that the Women's Studies department brought her to campus to read and conduct a work-shop. She began her presentation by saying, "I lie all the time, but my lies are always true." And she meant every word of it, and indeed her lies will burn the truth into you.

I remember Toni Cade as a funny, serious woman who said exactly what was on her mind, without concern about how it came out. Wiry, with a slender frame, a reddish Afro that had it own peculiar shape, Toni Cade talked with her entire body and it was clear that she was very comfortable in her skin. The sister was real, down-to-earth, bright yet humble, and a fabulous storyteller. She had me, and everyone else, captivated by her resonant voice, her effective pacing and the details of her stories. She had the audience enthralled, and it was evident that she was accustomed to and loved to entertain. I was honoured to be in her presence, and mesmerized by her constant motion, her wry sense of humour and her commitment to cultural work – which is what she said she as a Black writer/storyteller/video-maker has been and was continuing to be about, a cultural worker – a term which I have since used to apply to my role.

The finale of her residency was a performance reinterpreta-tion of "Goldilocks and the Three Bears", followed by a reading of her then unpublished novel, *If Blessings Come,*★ which was based on the disappearance/killings of the children of Atlanta in the late 1970s, but mostly it was about Black people who seemed to have abandoned collective concern for their children and who were not sufficiently outraged at such wanton crimes. In the novel, Toni Cade has the Atlanta children who were murdered talking to the Black community. Her reading chilled me to the marrow, left me stunned, ashamed, and thankful that she, this thin-boned woman who moved with a limp, was doing this work for all of us. It was then that I realized that Toni Cade Bambara was more than a writer/cultural worker; she epitomized what we Jamaicans call a "big woman", not because of size, but because of her heart, her independence, her willingness to go all the way, even alone. When she came off the stage, I hugged her, squeezed her hand and inquired when *If Blessings Come* would be published. I wanted every Black person to read it so we could begin the healing, undo the pain caused by the continuous loss, kidnappings, murderings, displacement. At the time, Toni Cade said she would see about publishing it, but that she was more interested in making video documents and that was where her energy was focused.

A year after Toni Cade's visit, I taught "African-American Women: History and Culture", and used *The Black Woman* (1970), the collection she edited, which garnered a great deal of debate from her essay, "On the Issue of Roles". In that very candid thesis she examines the role of Black women during the Civil Rights era, and relates that to how women's roles in Africa altered when the concept of property was introduced. My students and I spent a great deal of time debating the points in that essay. In other literature courses, I taught Bambara's *The Seabirds Are Still Alive*, 1974, but was and still am barely able to swim my way out of those stories. Her other novel, *The Salt Eaters*, 1980, sucks me in like a vacuum cleaner, causing near suffocation. Toni Cade Bambara can write her way in and out of a tale as judiciously as she can tell a story and have listeners spellbound. She speaks the truth in a way that is often painful to hear as it begs you, the reader, to act, to move beyond thought and/or passivity to activism. I continued to teach her work, mostly her stories, to other students at the University of California, Berkeley where I had then moved, and they too fell in love with her through her work. She remained ever present in my memory.

Then in 1992, Barbara Christian, a mutual friend, telephoned to inform me that Toni Cade was in the hospital with colon cancer, and asked that I light a candle for her and send her love. While she was still recuperating from surgery, I called and spoke with her, sending her my blessings and inquiring how I could assist. I was inspired by her brave tone and dauntless demeanour, which came across the telephone line. I followed up my call with a letter and a book of affirmation. I spoke with Toni Cade only a few times after that, and then sent her a flyer for an anthology on single mothers that I was editing, urging her to write a piece for the collection. She said she was doing better, but wasn't sure when she would be able to get to the piece on single parenting; however, she encouraged me to forge ahead. Toni Cade remained in my prayers and thoughts, but I did not speak to her after that.

Once again via the telephone, over a year later, I received news about her. Returning home late one night after a reading, messages on the answering machine from Barbara Christian and Joyce Carol Thomas informed me that Toni Cade was dead, and that a gathering to honour her passing was being planned. I replayed the messages twice, feeling as I listened that the world should pause to commemorate the transition of such a feisty and important Black woman writer. Then I went into my home-office and took down and read my favourite story, "The Lesson", and again thanked Toni Cade for teaching us all so many important lessons, foremost of which is that Black women must support each other.

While Karma, Toni's daughter, and others were united to celebrate the crossing over of this warrior in Philadelphia, a few of us writers gathered at Joyce Carol Thomas's home in Berkeley to remind ourselves that this sister/friend touched us, some of us intimately, others solely through her work. We assembled to affirm that we would not allow her to be forgotten because we would forever remember and hold her dear in our hearts. Barbara Christian, who had known Toni Cade since their days at City College in New York in the 1960s, read an excerpt from an essay she was working on about Bambara and affirmed her as a teller of tall tales. Joyce Carol recounted Toni Cade's visit to the University of Tennessee that she organized, and spoke of Toni Cade's love and concern for Karma, her daughter. Belvie Rooks remembered her laughter from meeting her when she was in residence at San Francisco State in 1984; Evelyn White recalled their meeting and their banter. Leona Welch said she had never met Toni Cade personally, but through the work her soulful spirit was evident. Elena Featherson was unable to make it but sent a letter that was read by Henri Norris who had been in close contact with Toni Cade most recently, discussing with her alternative treatments for cancer. Alice Walker spoke of their friendship and offered a memorable slice of Toni Cade. And there were others: Wanda Fox, Dorothy Tsuruta as well as her teenage daughter, Nikki, and Joyce's granddaughter, Maria Pecot, present to honour the passing of this remarkable human being who touched so many through her words. Everyone paid tribute to Toni Cade in their own way, and as a closure I retold Toni Cade's version of "Goldilocks and the Three Bears" a story full of the fond humour that I remember when I heard Toni Cade tell it for the first time.

Then we broke bread, shed tears and sat in silence with Sweet Honey in The Rock harmonizing, "There is a Balm in Gilead", in the background, helping us to ease our sister/writer/friend, Toni Cade Bambara's spirit on her journey. We were reluctant to part, pledged our commitment to each other and promised to keep Toni Cade Bambara alive through teaching and sharing her works with our students and friends.

December 9, 1995, the date Toni Cade Bambara, storyteller, writer and a generous spirit crossed over to another path will always remain sacred, and I am indebted to her for leaving us amazing stories and precious memories of her magnanimous spirit and zest for life.

⋆*Those Bones Are Not My Child*, her novel about the Atlanta children, was published posthumously, twelve years after her death under this title rather than her original, *If Blessings Come.*

LIFE OUTSMARTING DEATH:
BARBARA CHRISTIAN
(2000)

barbara be a talking
seeing   righteous
sister opening
our eyes
reading us like
a mirror

Poetry is sitting at the deathbed of a sister-friend, Barbara Christian, holding her hand, telling her I love you and watching her dying the way she lived, fighting, arguing with death, screaming at this rapist, serial killer who has taken her sisters earlier – Lorraine, Audre, Toni Cade, Shirley Ann, and now her. Barbara. Babs. Professor Christian. Poetry are the words that even now, with pain gnawing at her body, she tries to speak, an eloquent rambling that quilts our lives into a tapestry so large that no one can ignore us. Poetry is the hardest working, poetic loving, kicking-ass, trailblazing feminist who never gives up on her people, who sees around the corner to the good side.

Barbara Christian opened the door of the university wide and let many in; she trained scholars and critics, teachers and women how to fight for their own lives and speak their truths without apology. Professor Christian, the first African American woman to win tenure at the University of California, Berkeley, 1978, was the first to be promoted to full professor, 1986, and the first African American ever to receive the prestigious Distinguished Teaching Award, 1991. In 2000, she was awarded the university's highest honour, the Berkeley Citation. Barbara, whose house was always open to everyone, responded to every phone call, every e-mail, all requests for help and support. She was a literary critic, a mother, a mentor, a confidant, a scholar. She was always writing letters of recommendations for graduate students, colleagues for tenure, curriculum for teaching Black women's literature, writing.

barbara be a good time
generous sister
welcoming all
into a circle of knowing
and friendship
noncompetitive
enjoying banter
and dancing and singing along
        to bob marley

Poetry is Barbara writing, refusing to be silenced, her "Race for Theory" challenging the theorists who would attempt to displace and subordinate African American women writers. Barbara was the kind of poetry we need to hear and read. She made the revolution happen, not the armed-with-guns, folks-calling-out-their-names revolution that burns off quickly, and very little changes. She was always there for me and countless others, opening her home, my first book party, shower for first child, marriage ceremony, fortieth birthday. Supporting; there to chair my dissertation, to hood me. There for talks and talks and laughter and gardening and strategizing. Barbara. Advisor, friend, big sister. She was always there for me and sisters whose name she didn't know. Women from Germany, Italy, Africa, Japan and India came all the way to California to work and study with her. Giving of her time and self. I met her when she was in the midst of making final revisions to *Black Women Novelists, The Development of a Tradition, 1892-1976*, 1980. She made me/us know the tradition, that African American women were writers and poets and playwrights; she set the standard and paved the way for canonizing African American women writers.

barbara be a generous
doorkeeper
fiercely tenacious
laughing
dancing us into new spaces
debunking hierarchy
always down to earth

the caribbean mocking
her speech

Poetry is Barbara Christian, champion of black women writers, community activist, protesting the invasion of Grenada, fighting to get the university to divest in apartheid South Africa, working with women on welfare, bridging the gap between the academy and the community, integrating intellect and grassroots, creating more dialogue – *Black Feminist Criticism, Perspectives on Black Women Writers*, 1985 – continuing to push the literature into the mainstream as one of the senior editors of the *Norton Anthology of African American Literature*, 1997. Championing the works of Paule Marshall, Alice Walker, Toni Morrison, et al; advocating to get funds for students, protesting the university's position on Affirmative Action, never backing down, being eloquent and articulate, working long after everyone else had gone home. Travelling down new paths, working to establish a paradigm for feminist diaspora studies, Caribbean and African women writers. Barbara, you be what poetry is.

> you be
> one of us
> we be
> one of you
> you be
> keeping us on the path
> you be
> writing us
> free and safe
> you be
> our ancestor now.

Dr. Barbara Christian died from cancer at her home in Berkeley, California, on Sunday, June 25, 2000.

SHE BE THE SPIT AND THE FLAME: A TRIBUTE TO JUNE JORDAN
(2002)

In 1981, searching to find meaningful essays to use in teaching basic composition to students at San Francisco State University, I stumbled on *Civil Wars*, your collection of essays, June, and for many years it was my bible. I used the essays to introduce students to the politics and craft of essay writing. I taught the book from cover to cover numerous times, and other times, I taught only my favourite essays from it, "White English/Black English: The Politics of Translation" (1972). What I love about your essays, June, are their frank honesty and clarity of voice. "Language is political. And Language, its reward, currency, punishment, and/or eradication – is political in its meaning and its consequence" (72). June, you don't mince or hide behind words. You say exactly what you mean, letting the spit fly from your mouth.

> your tongue was aflame
> fire raged on its surface
> you curled it and spat out words
> orange and blue in heat
> you said what we wanted to say
> when we couldn't find the words
> your spittle doused our enemies
> and we welcomed your saliva as baptism

I had been reading your poetry all along. I had been reading your essays, and in 1984, when you came to check out UC Berkeley before relocating a few years later, Barbara Christian, your sister-friend in the struggle for women's studies and social justice, introduced us. You signed *Civil Wars* for me then, and I remember thinking how slightly built you were and how soft and gently you spoke in contrast to the heat of your essays. June, you smiled a lot and smoked and talked fast, and I liked you instantly as a sister, as we chatted about our Caribbean roots and South Africa and where the world was heading. You were everywhere at once, June – international, connecting struggles, some of which

I knew little about, so I listened, intoxicated by the breadth of your knowledge.

The next year, 1985, when *On Call* appeared, I bought and read it voraciously. Tears streamed down my face reading "Many Rivers to Cross", and I could hear the plaintive sounds of Jimmy Cliff's rendition of the song of the same title replaying in my head, soliciting more tears. And all the scenes and details, June, that you describe in "Nicaragua: Why I Had to Go There", I knew, and your voice gave sound to my thoughts before I was able to articulate them. You broke it all the way down for others and me, June, in the cold-blooded badass essay, "Nobody Mean More to Me than You and the Future Life of Willie Jordan". I envied your insight, precision, the direct simplicity with which you write, your words opening wide my eyes to see and know the full truth and facts of the matter. It was love I was feeling, reading those essays, June. It was your love for justice, for truth, for sharing. I could feel the blue flames like candle wicks extend from your fingers, marking the pages without destroying them, and the phlegm in my throat was coughed up, and I found my own words. Your words fed me a raging language.

> you read with a fevered passion
> a combustion of words that exploded
> into rhythmic intensity
> they had to hear you
> hear you we hear you
> galvanizing the community
> to demand fairness and just treatment
> you detonated apathy
> your words incandescent

I moved between your poems and your essays in a dance that was endless, circular, and encompassing. When I picked up *Things that I Do in the Dark, 1967-1977*, I was intrigued by the title and the suggestive pose on the jacket cover, but from the first poem, "Who Look at Me", dedicated to Christopher, your son, I knew you were writing with a torch held high, and this wasn't about the Olympics, and it wasn't about arson. I too had felt what

you wrote: "I am stranded in a hungerland / of great prosperity."
I tell you, June, every which way I turn, I feel your spittle like a
flashlight revealing the path on a starless night. So many times as
I read one of your essays, I wanted to ask you who fans your flame
to get it to the right heat. Often, after reading you, my memory
is flooded with this image of my paternal grandmother sitting on
a low stool on the back veranda, with a piece of cardboard fanning
the coals. After she blew on them – the red amber breaking
through the black – the coals were ready to roast sweet potatoes.
That's what "Not a Suicide Poem" is: coals igniting because, as
you aptly state, "no one should feel peculiar living / as they do."
We deserve more, at least in our own lives, deserve to be free from
police brutality, free from racism, sexism, homophobia, class and
religious dogma. We need to claim our own spaces and chant as
you chant, "I must become / I must become a menace to my
enemies."

> you mastered walking on fire
> your soles hardened by conviction
> your body became an impenetrable
> island around which we danced
> the call for rectitude
> collective individual
> and you spat out more poems
> sizzling the coals

Fighting your own battle, breast cancer, you did not hide, fold
in on yourself. Instead you garnered statistics: six women die
from breast cancer every hour, and you allowed your fear and
anger to surface: "And I am still at a loss about how I should wage
that battle for my life. / Nobody knows. And that totally pisses me
off. / I mean, like, why not? / One in eight women in the USA will
be diagnosed with invasive breast cancer: one in eight! / Every
year there are 1830 cases of breast cancer reported, in the USA,
and..." You sought treatment, weighed recommendations, agreed
to a mastectomy thinking the odds were in your favour, only to
be told you had a forty percent chance. And when you wrote and
spoke, "And I felt furious then. And I feel furious now. / And I felt

helpless then. / And I feel helpless now," we understood, especially those of us who had lost sisters and mothers, aunts and cousins, daughters and nieces, friends and acquaintances to this deadly killer. You have been fighting all along. Not just for yourself. You had a right to be tired, and we sent you love, silent prayers and blessed thanks because you had been our voice, an inferno in the malaise of cutbacks, affirmative action dismantling, widespread violence and general madness.

I am still working at being as brave as you in the face of personal violation. June, how did you learn to stand naked, vulnerable to attacks and criticism? Who taught you the language of bravery and how to recognize and shout out your voice? You knew statistics were good, but it is the personal stories that allow for transformation. So you testified. "Both times I was raped I was / by myself. / I was isolated. / I did not possess a manifesto / or an invisible-but-known-and-building / community." You protested apartheid and worked at forming communities, knowing that it was more than strength in numbers, it was our very lives, how we live, the joys we celebrate and the pain we share, that have everything to do with a lived community. It takes spit to light a flame. It takes love and caring. It takes doing the work and not hiding behind jargon. You, June, showed us what a working poet-activist looks like, what is possible.

And you have given us so much; titles too numerous to list. Even after flying off on the blue wind, you let us know, June, that you had not gone anywhere so we have *Some of Us Did Not Die* (2002), and you will never die. You live strong and tangible in the words, and after all isn't that the legacy that a poet-activist bequeats us? Where did you find the time, June, in sixty-five years to write so much, to know so much, to be the fire and the spit to inflame and extinguish? Each work widening the circle. Always embracing the world in your essays and poems, always global yet specific, always personal, yet communal, connecting more than dots. And in this triumphant, brave collection of yours, writing on September 25, 2002, "Do You Do Well To Be Angry?", after the World Trade Center was destroyed in New York, you share in the national grief and despair, but your pain is tempered with reason.

We have become a wilderness of jeopardized loved ones, and terrifying strangers.

I am an American.

I listen to our leaders calling for "the eradication of evil", and I am wondering, who among us is without evil?

What nation, what people, what stretch of my own personal history is good without blemish, without blame, without crimes of inertia, at least?

Was our firebombing of Dresden a terrorist attack?

Or Hiroshima?

Or the bombing of Beirut?

Or the bombing of Baghdad?

Is there anything for which we, as a nation, need to atone? (p. 37).

How in two weeks, June, in just two weeks, could you with your own personal struggle for your life, put words on paper and force us to see beyond the rubble and loss? How did you muster the courage to be our conscience and our foresight in the midst of your body's disintegration? Yet you remind us at the end of this piece that none of us is perfect, we are all flawed (you continuing to smoke even after surgery for cancer), but there are lessons to be learned. "And I hope we will learn, soon enough, that sometimes there is no difference. / Sometimes I am the terrorist I must disarm. / Sometimes I am the Penalty, and sometimes I am the Companion of the Fire" (p. 43). I am breathing, June. Taking deep breaths and looking closely at myself. Judging myself and my actions before I point a finger because I know I am often both the one who started the fire and the fire raging out of control. All too often, many of us are both.

Where are you now, June? Are you the bird I hear singing at my bedroom window? Are you that butterfly that flits in my garden, hovering near the apple tree? Or are you the soil, or that voice that won't leave me, that voice that summons me to write even after a long day and tiredness licks at my eyes? Where are you, June? It doesn't matter where. I believe you are everywhere, in every word, in all the many words you left us as a legacy, a testimony of your life and your commitment to humanity. You have passed the baton. Who now will take it and run as fast, and fiercely and resiliently as you? You who taught, mentored and encouraged, you who made your life an example.

> even after fire has extinguished
> itself ash remains
> a visible reminder of its power
> to transform
> your flame glows June Jordan
> your flame helps to light other torches
> your flame is a mirror
> your flame is your irrepressible spirit

I am so happy that I knew/know you. So happy that I was able to witness your love for justice, your desire for privacy, your need to give voice to social and political wrongs, your honesty in the face of exposure, your determination not to be a victim, your willingness to use your experiences to teach, to encourage, to offer hope, to dispel the lies. In *Passion: New Poems, 1977-1980*, you chanted what we all need to chant, living as we do in a world that would make us feel iniquitous, inferior, and forget our true selves: "I am not wrong: Wrong is not my name / My name is my own my own my own..."

ALSO BY OPAL PALMER ADISA

Caribbean Passion
ISBN: 9781900715928, pp. 96; pub. 2004, £7.99

Caribbean Passion is feisty, sensuous and thought provoking – everything one expects from Opal Palmer Adisa. Whether writing about history, Black lives, family, or love and sexual passion, she has an acute eye for the contraries of experience. Her Caribbean has a dynamic that draws from its dialectic of oppression and resistance; her childhood includes both the affirmation of parents that makes her 'leap fences' and the 'jeer of strange men on the street/that made your feet stumble'; and men are portrayed both as predators and as the objects of erotic desire.

This vision of contraries is rooted in an intensely sensuous apprehension of the physical world. She observes the Caribbean's foods and flora with exactness; makes them emblematic metaphors that are often rewardingly oblique; and uses them as starting points for engagingly conversational meditations on aspects of remembered experience. There is a witty play between food and sexuality, but counterpointing her celebration of the erotic, there is a keen sense of the oppression of the female body. In her poem 'Bumbu Clat', for instance, she explores the deformation of a word that originally signified 'sisterhood' to become part of the most transgressive and misogynist curse in Jamaican society. In this doubleness of vision, the term 'womanist' was invented to describe Opal Palmer Adisa's work.

'With *Caribbean Passion*, Adisa continues to challenge our perceptions of Caribbean life. Although the title and sensual cover image suggest a collection of steamy, romantic verse, many of these poems detail the region's turbulent history and chaotic present, suggesting an overriding resilience in the face of unspoken sexual abuse, lost Haitian refugees, and gender-based tyranny, all delivered in a unique and authentic voice.'

Dave Katz, *Caribbean Beat*

Until Judgement Comes: Stories about Jamaican Men
ISBN: 9781845230425, pp. 258; pub, 2007, £8.99

The stories in this collection move the heart and the head. They concern the mystery that is men: men of beauty who are as cane stalks swaying in the breeze, men who are afraid of and despise women, men who prey on women, men who have lost themselves, men trapped in sexual and religious guilt, men who love women and men who are searching for their humanity...

The stories are framed by the memories of an old Jamaican woman about the community that has grown up around her. The seven stories are structured around wise sayings that the community elder remembers as her grandfather's principle legacy, concerning the nature of judgement, both divine and human. Each story uses a saying as the starting point but the stories are far from illustrative tracts. From Devon aka Bad-Boy growing up with an abusive mother, to Ebenezer, a single man mysteriously giving birth to a child, to the womanizer Padee whose many women and children struggle to resolve issues with their father, each story reveals the complex, and often painful, introspective search of these men.

'With these seven fantastic stories, the essence of what it means to live and die as Jamaican men comes off the pages like virtual life in time gone by, not as historical references, but as continuous realities in the museum out of which every living Jamaican man has emerged... *Until Judgement Comes* will be a classic and deserves a place in the annals of transformative Caribbean literature.'

Winston Nugent, *The Caribbean Writer*

ABOUT THE AUTHOR

An award-winning poet and prose writer, Opal Palmer Adisa has eleven titles to her credit, including the novel, *It Begins With Tears* (1997), proclaimed by Rick Ayers as one of the most motivational works for young adults. She has been a resident artist in internationally acclaimed residencies such as Sacatar Institute (Brazil) and Headlines Center for the Arts (California, USA). Her work has been reviewed by Ishmael Reed, Al Young, and Alice Walker (*Color Purple*), who described her work as "solid, visceral, important stories written with integrity and love."

Following in the tradition of the African "griot", Opal Palmer Adisa is an accomplished storyteller who is much sought after for her inspirational work with children.

A teacher, diversity trainer, literary critic, and mother of three children, Opal is also the parenting editor and host of KPFA Radio Parenting show in Berkley, California. She has published numerous articles on different aspects of parenting, and is currently working on a parenting book.

Dr. Adisa is a full professor of creative writing and literature at California College of the Arts. She has taught at several universities including Stanford University and University of California, Berkley. Her poetry, stories, essays and articles on a wide range of subjects have been collected in over 200 journals, anthologies and other publications, including *Essence Magazine* (Feb. 2006) She has also conducted workshops in elementary through high school, museums, churches and community centers, as well as in prison and juvenile centers.

She was born in Jamaica.